LEAVING THE BOYS

Leaving
the Boys

A Story of Motherhood and Career,
Feminism and Romance

MINDY CAMERON

LUMINARE PRESS
WWW.LUMINAREPRESS.COM

Printed in the United States of America

Cover Design by Melissa K. Thomas

Luminare Press
442 Charnelton St.
Eugene, OR 97401
www.luminarepress.com

LCCN: 2020909271
ISBN: 978-1-64388-346-5

For Matt and Tim,
the boys

TABLE OF CONTENTS

LEAVING

December 28, 1976

"Hi, Dad," Matt and Tim said in unison as their father walked through the front door. I hung back.

"Hey, kids," Ken said as the three of them turned into the living room, still cluttered with Matchbox cars, Hot Wheels tracks, an unopened five-hundred-piece puzzle with a picture of the solar system on top. Ken gave me a quick over-the-shoulder glance, as if questioning what to do next. I stayed near the entryway, nodded, put out my hand, and, with a slight push of my fingers, encouraged him to go ahead and sit with the kids.

"Let's see what you've put in your new treasure chests," he said, moving to the far corner of the living room where I'd put the wooden boxes with their names carved on top. I'd asked a friend to make them—special going-away gifts that might become keepsakes.

"Nothin' yet," said Matt.

"My favorite's a blue Mustang," said Tim, kneeling to open the chest and show his dad the special car.

Nervous, I felt the minutes ticking by, checked my watch, then walked toward the sofa, along the wall opposite Ken and the boys. Ken looked my way and I pointed to the watch.

Evening had settled in, the little-used and sparsely furnished front room was nearly dark, lit by the single bulb on the floor lamp in the corner near the new boxes.

"Okay, guys, it's time to head out." The kids looked at me. "Really, Mom?" said Tim. "Yeah, I'm afraid so." I stood up and moved slowly toward the door.

Matt came over and gave me a quick hug. "Bye, Mom." Tim followed his lead, but held on longer, much longer. I leaned down and whispered in his ear, "I'll call as soon as I get there."

Ken tossed a glance and a goodbye wave my way and ushered the boys onto the front porch, into the night.

I closed the door behind them and stood there, my back pressing against that door for what seemed like a long time but may have been only seconds. Finally, I went to the wooden box with Tim's name on it, leaned over and pulled out the tiny blue Mustang. I held it, turned it around, inspecting it for the detailed reality that made Matchbox cars so popular with young boys. I placed the small car back in the otherwise empty chest and closed the lid.

Friends would be arriving soon to take me out to dinner on my last night in Boise. I turned out the light in the front room, looked around my dark house, and imagined what it would look like in a few days, after Ken moved back in with the boys. I noticed the bedraggled philodendron hanging in its basket in the dining area. I walked past the table, the center of family time with the boys, and went to the kitchen sink for a glass of water. While feeding the thirsty plant, I caught sight of the new photograph sitting on the windowsill, the one taken just a few months before. It was a close-up of me and the boys, smiling, against a bright blue sky and tree branches that had lost most of their leaves. A duplicate was already tucked away in my luggage, destined to travel with me when I left the next morning. I reached out to touch their faces, Matt's dark curls, Tim's light-brown, shaggy hair.

Women have always left their children, but it's usually out of desperation—abuse, depression, poverty. As a young woman in Boise, I was not desperate; I was determined to change my life, a determination fueled by the intensity of new love, desire to pursue a budding career, and an independent spirit set free by the emergent feminist movement.

The doorbell rang. Quickly, I gathered my coat and purse—so ready for the diversion my friends would provide this final evening before leaving Boise and the boys.

GRADUATION

1965

I walked into the doctor's office across the street from campus and, at first glance, thought, "Oh, shit!"

"You're Mindy, right?" said the receptionist, a pleasant, gray-haired woman I recognized as the wife of Professor Rowe, my journalism teacher and advisor, the person I least wanted to know about this appointment. "The doctor can see you now," she said.

Commencement at Pacific University, a small, liberal arts school twenty miles west of Portland, was just two months away. I was one of four journalism students graduating this year. Although I didn't have a job lined up—hadn't tried yet, really—Professor Rowe and I were both confident that, with my grades and newspaper experience, exciting opportunities awaited.

After doing a brief exam, the doctor confirmed my suspicions. "Yes," he said, "you're pregnant."

And so it began, my fall from grace into a cloudy future and a present filled with embarrassment and shame. The depth of those feelings—so new to me—would overwhelm me in a few days, but first I had to absorb the shock of the doctor's words. Even though I had suspected this, the realization—*I'm going to have a baby!*—induced an out-of-body experience. I was two different people. The old me, the one about to graduate, the one with a promising but still unknown future, was falling into an abyss. The new me, the pregnant one leaving the doctor's office, stood outside the door in the bright, chilly sunlight of a March day, staring across the street to the campus oak trees, wondering what to do next.

In high school I'd known of girls who had disappeared and returned many months later. The gossip was that they had gone away to have a baby and give it up for adoption. I was not a high school girl who "got in trouble." I was a twenty-two-year-old with a twenty-four-year-old boyfriend. We were both about to graduate from college, me with a bachelor's degree in journalism and political science, he as a ready-to-practice optometrist. We hadn't talked about a future together. Until that day, I was imagining a life after college that did not include my boyfriend, Ken. Instead, I imagined a career in journalism or government. I had only vague assumptions about an eventual marriage and children.

As strange as it may seem today, I had never heard about abortion, probably because it was illegal, and I was living in the sheltered environment of Pacific University and Forest Grove. Portland seemed a world away, past forested rolling hills, wheat fields, dairy farms, hazelnut orchards and strawberry patches. The Supreme Court decision *Roe v. Wade*, which legalized abortion and changed everything for the next generation of women, was still eight years into the future.

Walking across campus to my dorm, I saw no avenue for running away from this predicament. In my small world, if you got pregnant you got married.

Wanting some time to let my new reality—pregnancy, marriage—soak in, I kept the news to myself for a while. Talking to Ken could wait. I stayed in my room all afternoon, skipping dinner and seeing no one while I plotted the next steps. After a night of tossing and turning, I got up and dressed slowly, in no hurry for what came next. Clouds had moved in overnight, and it was cold and damp as I trudged to the ratty house Ken shared with four friends across the street, on the north edge of campus. Ken and I didn't routinely hang out there, usually going off somewhere more private, but I'd shared a few pizzas and hamburgers around the table and liked his housemates.

I knocked once, lightly, and the door opened. It was a fellow optometry student, a guy from Hawaii I liked very much. "Hi. Is Ken here?"

"Come on in," he said. "It's cold out there." I slipped inside. "Hey, Ken, you got a visitor." Soon Ken walked into the room, smiling as he saw me. "Hi there. What's up?"

I couldn't muster a smile. "I need to talk to you. Can we go someplace else?"

"My room okay?"

The room was messy with clothes on the floor, rumpled sheets and an old greenish-brown Army blanket tossed over the lumpy mattress. The blind was drawn on the lone window, allowing narrow slits of tree-shaded light into the room. The only other illumination came from a small bedside lamp. We sat on the edge of the bed.

"I'm pregnant," I said in a flat, low voice, staring at the floor.

A quick intake of breath, then a slow release. "How do you feel about that?" he said.

"Lousy, really, really, lousy. How could we be so careless?" I wasn't blaming him. After stewing all night, I wasn't in the mood for blaming. I'd accepted the reality that we shared the responsibility for carelessness about using condoms. Only later did I learn about the oral contraceptive, widely known as "the pill," which had been approved in 1960. By 1965, millions of women were using it, presumably married women, as it was illegal for unmarried ones. That didn't change until 1972.

Ken reached out to put his arms around me and pull me to his side for a hug. "Well, it sure is a surprise, but I'm not all that unhappy about it," he said. I took no comfort from his closeness and remained still, not leaning into him or returning his hug. I sat motionless in the gloom, staring at the grimy, worn carpet.

Finally, I raised my head, sat up straight, took a deep breath and looked at Ken. "I sure wish I could feel that way, but I don't. Anyhow, we have to figure some things out."

I had already figured things out overnight, and I proceeded to tell him my ideas: Elope as soon as possible, find a place to live near campus and plan for summer and beyond. Ken was not resistant to any of this; in fact, his smile made it seem he was happy about it and willing to humor me by going along with my plans.

I insisted on getting married as soon as possible in another county to avoid having our marriage-license information appear in the local newspaper. I knew from my summer stints working at a small-town newspaper that most of them published births, deaths, and marriages in small type in the legal section. Many readers look through those columns to find familiar names. I didn't want mine to be one of them. We decided to go to Gresham, on the east side of Portland in Multnomah County. Later, I checked and was told we didn't need to bring witnesses because clerks there were always willing to watch and sign the papers.

Getting there was a dilemma. Gresham was nearly forty miles away, and neither of us had a car. Ken asked around about borrowing from a friend, but nothing came of that. My back-up plan was to borrow my mother's car, a small, baby-blue Studebaker called a Lark. I had used it a few times before, but Mom always seemed a little hesitant.

As soon as the phone rang my mouth went dry. "Hi, Mom, it's Mindy."

"I know that," she said, exasperated. She knew each daughter's voice instantly and was peeved when we identified ourselves.

"Hey, I'm hoping I can use your car for a day or so week after next." And then I lied: "I have a meeting in Portland with some other girls from campus, and no one has a car. We'd really appreciate it." I gave her the date and she checked her calendar.

"Well, I guess that will be okay." I detected reluctance. I knew she liked the independence of having her own car around for whatever might come up—a trip to the grocery store, ferrying younger daughters around. Unaccustomed to lying to her, I closed my eyes and felt my face flush with a renewed sense of shame as I thanked her and uttered a soft goodbye.

My desire for secrecy, even with my parents, grew out of bottomless remorse and embarrassment about the mess I had gotten myself into. Telling friends and Professor Rowe would be hard enough; I could hardly bear the thought of telling my parents. Waiting for the scheduled day in Gresham just allowed more time for me to burrow deeper within myself and wallow in regret. I told no one about the pregnancy, not even my best

Mindy Cameron

friend, Laura, and I didn't share my feelings with Ken. What would I say? I had no words to explain how I was feeling.

Years later, I began to refer to these days as the start of my "brain-dead period," but that description is not quite right. My brain was very much alive, actively making plans; it was my heart that shut down. As I drew inward, I lost my self-confidence and wiped from my imagination old dreams of the future—a newspaper job or government work in Washington, DC. Before I learned of my pregnancy, I'd interviewed on campus with representatives for government agencies, including the CIA, and gotten positive feedback, which created a short-lived bubble of optimism about future opportunities. The bubble burst and for weeks I lived day to day, numb to emotions, just doing what had to be done—school, preparation for graduation, a summer job. Ken tried, but failed, to jolly me out of my depression. He seemed not to share my regrets about getting married and resorted to a few stock jokes and nicknames. We'd met when I was serving milk on the cafeteria line, and he liked to call me Mindy Moo. Ken just being his normal self was aggravating to me, and I reacted by freezing him out. He didn't seem to notice, but probably I was the one not noticing. I know now how unkind and unfair my coolness was, but at the time I seemed incapable of ordinary human feelings.

The marriage in Gresham came off as planned, including the accommodating clerks. My plan for returning Mom's blue Lark was to take Ken back to campus and go home alone. I knew Mom and Dad had never warmed to Ken—his occasional grammatical missteps and Mormon background—and I thought breaking the news to them without him there would be easier for all of us. I parked the car in the driveway and found Mom in the kitchen.

"Hi, Mom, thanks for the car. Where's Dad? There's something I need to tell you about."

"The car? Did you have an accident?" Mom asked.

"No, the car's fine. It's something else, and it's important."

My little sister, Chris, then twelve, had come up from the basement to see what was going on. "Maybe you better go back downstairs," Mom told her as Dad, who had seen the blue Lark, came in from working in the yard.

We stood near the table in the nook by the kitchen. I was jittery and reached out to hang onto the back of a chair; I didn't want to bother sitting down. "So, here's the news," I said, delivering it like the lead of a newspaper story. "Ken and I are married. We just eloped, and I'm pregnant."

Stunned silence. Finally, Dad barked, "Where's Ken? Why isn't he here?"

"I asked him not to come. I wanted to do this by myself. I know it's a shock. It's been a shock for me, too, and for Ken, of course."

Dad wouldn't accept that explanation. "Well, he should be here. He should not have let you do this alone."

Mom sat down and slapped her hands on the table. "This is what you borrowed my car for?" She was indignant, as if allowing me to use her car made her an accessory to all this. "And now you are married, expecting a baby! What will you do? When is the baby due? Why didn't you talk to us *first*?" She was hurt and angry. A mother left out of a daughter's life-changing decision.

"I'm sorry, Mom. I just needed to do this my way." I was hollowed out emotionally and incapable of providing her any comfort. Instead of hugs and tears, I filled them in on the next steps for me and Ken. I would move into his room at the house across from campus while we looked for a cheap apartment for the summer. Ken had lined up a job at the cannery in Forest Grove; I would work at the newspaper in nearby Hillsboro. Ken had contacted the army to see about enlisting and going to officer candidate school. The baby was due in November.

BIRTH

O n a beautiful spring day a few weeks later, Dad
drove out to Forest Grove to see me. I met him in
front of the crummy house where Ken lived with
his friends and now also me. It was not a place I wanted to
invite Dad into, so we sat in his car. He turned to look at
me, putting his arm across the top of the seat back. "As you
can guess," he said, "your mother and I have been thinking
a lot about your situation. We're worried about you."

"I know, Dad," I said, looking through the windshield
to the nearby tree branches swaying in the warm breeze.
"But I'll be okay."

"We'd just like you to think about something," he said,
and then outlined an alternative scenario: End the marriage,
move back home, find a job, and let them help raise the baby
as I got my life together.

I wasn't expecting this but took only a few seconds to
respond. "Gosh, Dad, I can't imagine doing that." Not a
thank-you, not a let-me-think-about-it, just quick rejection.

Years later I realized it was a generous offer, made with
loving intentions. But twenty-two-year-old me couldn't
absorb any of that. As I opened the car door and told Dad
goodbye, I assured him I knew what I was doing, and turned
to go back inside the ramshackle house.

The next months, including life with Ken and his room-mates, were largely lost in the fog of depression. Surely Professor Rowe and I had a conversation, but I have no recollection of it. Surely, I told my best friend, but I don't remember anything about it. I know I went through the commencement ceremony, but I remember nothing, including whether my parents attended, although I'm sure they did.

When Ken and I moved into a tiny attic apartment in an attractive but slightly shabby old home several blocks from the university, our marriage finally seemed real, even though I continued to feel more like a roommate than a newlywed. The marriage, the baby, the move—none of it engendered a new closeness or romance; I was merely executing a plan.

It was there we got the news that Ken was accepted for officer candidate school. It was unlikely that as an army optometrist he would be sent to Vietnam, but another overseas assignment was a possibility, and that is what he requested. Our plan—my plan—was playing out. The prospect of three years of a steady income in the military gave us a sense of financial security for the first time in our brief marriage.

I was still struggling with the loss of my sense of self, however. As my pregnancy become more obvious, I dreaded walking through town for fear I'd run into someone I knew. I rarely saw Laura and her husband, who lived in Forest Grove, and had little contact with my mother or sisters. I retreated into my childhood habit of finding contentment in being alone at home with a good book. I don't remember thinking about the baby or its stages of development. There were no ultrasounds then. I was healthy and didn't have any morning sickness; other than my growing belly, I was not constantly reminded of my pregnancy.

As a youngster I'd seen Mom pregnant and then bring a baby sister home from the hospital without a lot of commotion. That's how I wanted it to be for me. One unusually hot day in late October, I got a burst of energy and cleaned the apartment as I'd never cleaned it before—sweating through the heat of the day as I attacked floors, bathroom, closets, and clutter under the kitchen sink. A primitive nesting instinct must have overtaken me.

A week later, on November 6, a boy we named Matthew Scott was born. My shut-down heart opened. As it is with most new parents, it was love at first sight.

Not long before Matt's birth we had learned that our military assignment would be Vicenza, Italy. I was thrilled. An exciting future far away and a beautiful baby brought moments of joy into my life for the first time since that cool spring day in the doctor's office.

MATT WAS SIX WEEKS OLD WHEN I MOVED BACK HOME with my parents while Ken completed officer training in El Paso. In two months, we would depart for Italy. Mom and Dad seemed pleased to have me there, but for me it was awkward. Since the day I surprised them with my news, I'd felt distant from them, partly because of my own embarrassment and shame, but mostly because I hadn't had a close relationship with either of them during my high school and college years. I'd grown up and away, into a different world, imagining a life very unlike theirs. I had no sense then of the looming wave of feminism, or that my dreams of self-determination were roiling in young women like me across the country; all I knew was that my life would not be like my mother's. Going home, even for this short interval, seemed a surrender of that emergent new self. Now I see clearly the values of family and community ties I took from them, but back then, I didn't think about that, and conversation did not come easily, except with Mom about Matt and his care.

One day while preparing lunch I put Matt in the baby seat on the kitchen counter. Suddenly, the seat tipped and sent my baby tumbling to the floor on the opposite side of the counter. I rushed to pick him up off the floor in the cramped space between the family dining table and the counter. He was crying, of course, and I—who never panic—panicked. I held him tightly as thoughts of death or permanent damage to my beautiful boy raced through my mind. Mom came into the room and I blurted out what had happened. She took a quick look at Matt and reminded me that babies have soft heads and are not easily damaged.

"Take him to the rocking chair and hold him close," she said. I carried him into the light-filled living room, to the rocking chair where baby sisters had been soothed over the years. He soon calmed down, and the crying stopped; instead he whimpered like a kitten, a pitiful, blaming sound that seemed directed at me, his foolish, careless mother. He was falling asleep. Was it okay that he slept? Would he wake up? I continued rocking, dwelling on two thoughts: I had hurt my tiny infant, and I was a terrible mother. I was frightened and deeply remorseful, rocking and rocking like a metronome. Mom came around the corner from the kitchen to tell me she had called the doctor, who suggested we bring him in just to make certain he was all right.

We got into her blue Lark for the short drive to the doctor's office, me clutching Matt while Mom drove. The doctor found nothing to be alarmed about, repeated Mom's words about babies' soft heads, and, looking straight at me, assured me he would be fine. "Pay close attention over the next few days." And, he said with a smile, "Try not to drop him again."

Mindy Cameron

KEN

1961–1965

A s a high school senior contemplating college, I saw a brochure about Pomona College and harbored a secret desire to attend a school like that—a small, liberal-arts college in another state. Neither of my parents had gone to college, nor had my two older sisters. Although Mom and Dad supported my desire, I knew there was little money to pay for it. I was the third of seven daughters, and money for tuition was not in the family budget. With the help of my high school journalism teacher, a Pacific University graduate, I wound up at her alma mater twenty miles from home.

Pacific wasn't Pomona, but within weeks I felt so far from home I might as well have been in California. I arrived on the small, tree-studded campus of about six hundred students, a shy, naïve eighteen-year-old who had never been kissed and never heard the word *fuck*. At home, my parents' liberal politics masked conservative social attitudes grounded in the postwar forties and fifties. Moms worked in the home, neighborhoods were homogeneous, and fathers toiled hard to support the family. Children behaved and girls looked forward to marriage. Like many parents of that era, my folks were ill equipped for the cultural revolution of the sixties and seventies. And so was I.

I loved college. At that time Pacific didn't have much of a reputation; it was one of several small, private liberal-arts colleges in western Oregon, distinguished then only for having an optometry school. Once I settled into the dormitory and began to make friends and attend classes, Pacific's reputation—or lack of one—didn't matter to me. Classes were invigorating, sometimes even inspiring. I was introduced to John Updike's fiction and to modern poetry, Greek tragedies, botany, and world history. Early social life was a whirlwind that included meet-and-greet dances between freshmen and sophomores. One dance partner held me so tight I could feel his erection pushed against me. Even naïve girls know this instinctively when they feel it for the first time. I was surprised, but not repelled. The first stirrings of a college girl's sexual awakening.

My first dates were with Russell, a tall, quiet, good-looking Chinese boy. Pacific had begun to recruit students from Hawaii, so people of Asian descent were not unusual on campus. Russell, however, was from California, not Hawaii. Our dates in the first months of college consisted of walks through the neighborhoods of Forest Grove, in a time of calm and budding friendship away from the campus frenzy. We talked about our families and high schools. He bent down and kissed me, and I responded. We took more walks and practiced kissing in the dark shadows of over-hanging tree branches and secluded street ends. Russell left Pacific after the first semester. By then our relationship had cooled, and I never knew why he left or where he went. He remains an almost mystical memory of my first months at college and my first kiss. When I return to Pacific, I often walk through those same leafy neighborhoods south of campus and think of Russell.

Skip, my on-again, off-again boyfriend from high school, had asked that we remain in touch after we went off to college, and that we get together over Christmas break. By the middle of fall semester, I knew that any ongoing relationship between us was impossible. I was immersed in the small world of Pacific, including an active social life. I wrote to Skip and told him I was moving on and he should do the same. He wrote back that he still wanted to see me at Christmas. At the end of our evening together during the holiday break, Skip handed me an envelope and leaned over for a goodbye kiss. He opened his car door and I opened mine; he stumbled as he walked me to the front door of the family home on Coleman Street, a bright young man my mother always thought was a great catch. He returned to the car. Inside, I opened the envelope. It included a large portrait photo of Skip, a very handsome young man, a forty-five-rpm record titled "Mindy" (a love song he had composed for me), and a beautiful love letter. It was touching beyond anything I could imagine. I cared more for him at that moment than any time during our dating years. Later, I followed his success as he went on to an illustrious career in music.

I BEGAN DATING KEN DURING MY SECOND SEMESTER AT Pacific. Two years older, a flirtatious slow talker with dreamy brown eyes and a long dating history, he had been pursuing me for several months. At first, I resisted, sensing he was not right, a little on the wild side for a "good girl" like me. At the same time, all of that was part of the attraction. I was a college coed now, ready to broaden my horizons and try new experiences. Ken invited me to a fraternity house party.

"Here, try this," Ken said. "It's sloe gin, a good starter drink."

Does anybody drink sloe gin anymore? It's not one of Britain's finest exports. A sloe is often referred to as a small plum, but in pictures it looks more like a blueberry. It grows in British hedgerows; when juices of the sloe are infused with gin and a bit of sugar, it winds up as a bright red liquor with a high alcohol content—15 to 30 percent, more often on the high side. I remember the sweet taste and, after a second glass—or was it a third?—a dizzy alcoholic haze. Soon I was carefully picking my way down the back stairs off the second-floor fire escape to the alley behind the fraternity house. I vomited, sat down under a tree, and was feeling a tiny bit better when Ken found me.

"Are you okay?"

"Yeah, I guess, but don't ever give me that sloe gin stuff again. I feel awful."

We dated off and on throughout college. Occasionally, my sense that he was not right for me would re-emerge, and I would call it off. Most of the other boys I would have liked to date were in the same fraternity and steered clear out of deference to Ken—at least that's what I told myself. Perhaps the truth is closer to who I was at twenty years old, a young woman with a cool exterior. Somehow Ken had cracked through that. During one period when we were not dating, I saw Ken on campus in the company of a notorious "fast" girl. I suspected it was a ploy to make me jealous, which Ken later confirmed, and it worked. Hormones were a real danger on college campuses, back then as much as today. We got back together, seriously so.

I lost my virginity on a sunny afternoon after slipping away with Ken from a lazy, beer-filled fraternity picnic in the countryside to a quiet, private spot in tall, grassy weeds. I'm not sure I said yes, or that he asked. We didn't know about those protocols back then. It happened. I was dazed by the whole incident—the beer and the sex—but, ultimately, not upset, and considered it a private matter, not something to chat about with friends, and certainly not my mother. A few furtive encounters in the roomy backseat of a forties-era Plymouth followed, and I soon realized I enjoyed sex.

Ken grew up the middle child in a Mormon family of five in Pocatello, Idaho. He was the black sheep of the family, fallen away from the church, called a "Jack Mormon" in parts of Idaho and Utah that are heavily influenced politically and culturally by the prevalence of the Church of Jesus Christ of Latter-Day Saints. He was proud of having escaped that influence and was attracted to me as another independent thinker. One thing about Ken was a little off-putting—he made grammatical errors in speech, "he don't" instead of "he doesn't," for instance. Later, after I met his family and other LDS from southern Idaho, I realized his speech pattern—what I first saw as imperfections—was not unusual; perhaps it was even a cultural trait. Ken, however, with less than perfect grammar and a slow speaking style, did not make a good impression with my parents. I didn't care. I was having a heady experience at college, and dating Ken was part of it. He was a good dancer, and with an awkward year as a high school cheerleader behind me, I learned the swing and the lindy hop, and always looked forward to the next campus dance. When the limbo craze of the early sixties came along, we tried that. Ken could go lower than I.

Looking back, I see a young woman, still studious, beginning to emerge from her shell, no longer the unknowing girl from a suburban settlement called Cedar Mill. My thoughts about the future were nothing more than hazy notions of a meaningful job in journalism or government, but I did not see Ken in that haze.

By our final semester in 1965, the picture in my mind was coming into focus. I was looking forward to finding a job and testing myself beyond the known perimeters of a small campus. As a job backup, I had taken the courses necessary to get a teaching certificate. The course work was a lot easier back then, and jobs were plentiful, but teaching was not something I imagined doing. Campus career day interviews fueled a dream of someday having a job in Washington, DC. If that didn't work out, I was confident that with Professor Rowe's help I could find a newspaper job in the Northwest.

Ken was facing the end of his college draft deferment as the Vietnam War buildup was underway. Despite our intimate relationship, we had never discussed marriage. To this day I do not know if Ken was imagining me in his future. I knew he wanted to go back to Idaho and practice optometry, just as he knew my hopes for a newspaper job or government service. Our failure to talk openly about going our separate ways seems odd to me now, but neither of us was introspective about ourselves or our relationship, and we somehow avoided what in retrospect seems an obvious conversation.

REMEMBERING

I climbed the ladder to the spacious attic above the garage and shop building that dominates the property my husband Bill and I own in rural north Idaho. Ignoring the layers of dust and bug carcasses littering the wood floor, I surveyed the cluttered space. Where is that box? I saw cartons full of books, old tapes, knickknacks and framed photographs—the usual collection of a life put in storage—stacked helter-skelter. Finally, way in the back, there it was—the box that held my journals, including a special one where I recorded the weeks leading up to the day I left my boys in Boise.

I lugged the box down the ladder and hauled the journals up the steep driveway to our house on the hill. Sunlight streamed through the windows as I sat on the sofa with the journals at my feet. I took out the fancy one, a gift in my early teens from an uncle whose job as a navigator for an international airline took him to exotic places. The cover was silver brocade imprinted with images of cranes, their wings widespread among red flowers. Inside, the thick, cream-colored pages were edged with gold. I have no idea why my uncle picked this book for me, one of seven sisters, all of whom got presents that day. I may have been known in the family as the bookish daughter, but I had never kept a diary, nor could he have known me as a dreamy girl with fantasies of the future, which I certainly was not. Still, this book was special, something I could hold in my hand, a promise of distant tomorrows that I might want to write about. The book became part of a meager collection of keepsakes I carried with me for the next twenty-five years—to college in Oregon, to Italy as a military wife with two small boys, to Lewiston, Idaho, and, finally, to Boise, and the occasion that compelled me to open the gilt-edged pages and capture events with words. This was the book I'd been searching for.

I leaned back into the sofa, took a deep breath, and looked up at the high peak of the wood-paneled ceiling of this house I love, readying myself for immersion into a time when all of this—the house, the property, a shared life in north Idaho—was unimaginable. The pages were coming unglued from the spine, but they remained firm, as firm as the life decisions I recorded on them: I would leave my children in Boise with their father, my ex-husband, Ken, and move to Rochester, New York, where I had a new job and where the man I loved had moved for his own new job. The first entry was dated November 13, 1976, the day Bill left: ...*A painful departure for both of us.* Further down the page: *I think the kids are beginning to accept my going.* During the six weeks between Bill's departure and mine, I chronicled the thoughts and tugs of emotions triggered by my decision. December 22: *Not once have I had a second thought, a moment of regret, even doubt, about what I am doing.*

No regrets, no doubts. That was then. What about now? Can I say that today? I stood up, moved to the tall, sliding-glass doors and looked out to the small lake below and forested hills beyond. The day was chilly, bright, and still.

I HAVE READ MANY STORIES BY WOMEN COMPELLED TO write because of awful things that happened to them. Nothing terrible happened to me. My story is about choices. It's about circumstances of time and place, and probably genetic good luck, all of which allowed me to overcome an early setback and choose an unconventional path with ramifications for me and my children. It wasn't all rosy; my choices set in motion years of struggle and separation, disappointments, and crises—but also personal and professional successes, the joy of intimacy, and rollicking good times with family and friends.

That day in the attic, Barack Obama was a second-term president, women filled many important roles in his administration, and there was talk of a post racial period in America. I was even imagining a woman in the White House after the next election. Before retiring at age fifty-eight from the *Seattle Times*, I had been editorial page editor for more than a decade and had written opinion columns, often about politics and women. I left in 2001. I was happy to be out of the fray, but there is no leaving behind the impulses of a political news junkie, even after moving to rural north Idaho. As a youngster I was raised on talk of Adlai Stevenson, presidential candidate in 1956. Dwight Eisenhower (Ike) won that year; I was thirteen years old and have been politically attuned all the years since.

As I write this, Donald Trump is an impeached president who dodged removal from office by a Senate unwilling to hold him accountable for bribing Ukraine to help him in his next election. He survived impeachment only to fail the leadership test posed by the national health crisis during the pandemic of the coronavirus. He is a man with no allegiance to the truth or science, no sense of history or appropriate presidential demeanor—the exact opposite of his predecessor. And, oh yes, Trump is an admitted sexual harasser. Perhaps that truth about Trump is one reason stories about sexual harassment and assault became so prevalent in the news. Trump's election seems to have inoculated him, but other powerful guys are no longer immune. There is greater incentive than ever to call out the bad behavior. Infuriating allegations about powerful men—in Hollywood, media, politics, Silicon Valley—remind me of my own experiences many years ago. They were not as crass as those described in many of today's stories, but in Boise of the early seventies, where I was a newspaper reporter and, later, worked for the local public television station, sexism was very real. I dealt with my share, from the institutional sexism of unequal pay and needing my soon-to-be ex-husband's signature for a car loan, to the personal—a few groping episodes by well-known and powerful men.

I was more puzzled than angered by those overtures, confused about what, if any, role I had in what was happening to me. Once, in 1974, while I was interviewing a U.S. congressman on live television, he moved his leg next to mine. I pulled away and he widened the spread of his legs to apply more pressure to mine. There was no confusion about the touching. I turned icy and hurried the interview to conclusion. Afterward, the congressman invited me to a cocktail party. In my anger and embarrassment all I could muster was a frosty "no thanks." I was flustered and ill prepared to respond, which has left embers of rage easily stoked all these years later into new sparks of anger and disgust. How refreshing it has been, finally, to hear more women speaking out and to see hard-working journalists find and write their stories.

———————————

BOISE WAS WHERE I BROKE FREE AND STARTED ON THE path that led to the *Seattle Times*, but this story starts much earlier. I see that breakaway impulse in my early years, as I tried to find my way to independence as a young girl in a big family, daughter number three in a family of seven girls. When I was growing up in the Fifties, big families were not as unusual as they are today, but a family with all girls? We were outliers. People would ask—or just assume—we were Catholic, which we were not. Although we attended a Congregational church during my growing-up years, religion played little direct role in family life. During adolescence I harbored a mix of pride and self-consciousness about my family, which seemed odd to me—weird, but interesting.

With sixteen years separating the oldest and youngest sisters, outings as a complete family were rare. The only occasion I remember was when Mom and Dad took us out to lunch at a seafood restaurant on the Oregon coast with windows overlooking the surf. Dad spoke to the hostess, and we watched while she directed servers to push two tables together where we could enjoy the view. As she escorted us to our seats, I felt other diners turn to look at us. I saw their lips move as they counted, their eyes widening as they got to seven. Mom and Dad were smiling, pleased to show off their daughters. My little sisters, giggling with delight, interested only in the ocean, not other diners, rushed to get seats closest to the window. Judy, the eldest, was her usual poised self, holding her head high and looking straight ahead, oblivious to the antics of the little girls and acting as if she were accustomed to dining out. I felt awkward, slightly embarrassed, sort of liking but mostly disliking the looks and whispers. Today I wonder about those mixed feelings. I was a shy preteen and lacked Judy's self-confidence. She was pretty with bright blue eyes and curls that hung softly; I had frizzy curls, and when I looked in the mirror, I saw squinty eyes and dorky hair. I was many years away from being comfortable in social settings, and I still think of myself as reserved, even shy. Others have called me cool or distant. Newsrooms have a way of hardening people, however, and others who've known me during and since those years have used the word *intimidating*—which is a far cry from how I see myself. A daughter-in-law once confessed that for a time, before she became part of the family, she thought I was a little intimidating. Today I chalk it up to a combination of my natural reserve, my former position of influence as an editor, and that I didn't smile enough as I went about my job. Also, survival in a newsroom can foster a coarseness—cussing, quick decisions, sarcasm, and harsh judgments—all of which I learned too well. In my life after newspapers, I have worked hard to shed that layer, well, all but the sarcasm, which seems to have come with the family genes.

I was a tomboy and a bookworm. But something more was going on inside my head and lay dormant until one afternoon in the basement laundry room with Mom. When my desire to climb trees waned, I still liked physical exertion, which I found in gym class. As a sixth grader, I loved my gym teacher, Mrs. Timmerman, a middle-aged woman with a ruddy complexion, whose energy and happy spirit injected a bright spot to my school day. Once, in our basement laundry room, I was folding clothes as Mom filled the washer. We talked about school and I told her how much I liked that class. "When I grow up, I think I might like to be a gym teacher like Mrs. Timmerman." Mom pulled out a load of wet clothes, dropped them into a basket and turned to look at me.

"Do you? I can't really see you doing something like that."

I stopped folding and stared at her. "Gee, Mom, why not? What do you think I should be?"

"Well, you *could* be a teacher for a while, maybe English, not gym classes."

"Oh, Mom, that sounds so boring."

She told me I might feel different when I was older. Then this: "You know what I've always thought you would be when you grow up? A wife and mother."

I didn't react at the time to what Mom said, but later I wondered why she would see me as "a wife and mother," a future that I had not imagined for myself. I hadn't shown any special interest in taking care of baby sisters as they came along. My sister Becky was seventeen months older than I, and that was her thing. The only dolls I liked when I was little were paper dolls; Esther Williams, the famous swimmer, was my favorite. Becky and I would cut out the costumes for our dolls, store them in a shoebox, and occasionally take them out and try on the different outfits. When we outgrew paper dolls, instead of playing "house," we played "office." We had found some old bookkeeping ledgers and receipt tablets with carbon paper for making copies, set up an office with a table and chairs, and imagined we were "office people." Where that came from is a mystery to me. No one we knew worked in an office, and we didn't watch much television.

Why would Mom imagine the grown-up me as a mother? Today I see it as the trap of the culture of the 1950s, an era that limited the imagination of many mothers, able to see for their daughters only what they experienced themselves. The result was a growing distance between us. I never forgot my disappointment in the discovery of her limited expectations, and I rarely turned to her for advice.

Years later, I learned that Mom's father had insisted she go to college, despite her objections. She wanted to be a nurse. To please her father, she enrolled in college, but also bought nursing uniforms, hoping to pursue her dream after satisfying her father's wishes for a year. Neither college nor nursing school was in her future, however. Mom, the eighth of nine children, was close to her mother, who was in ill health, and Mom stayed home to care for her. When her mother died at age fifty of heart disease, my mother soon married—a nice young man her brothers approved of—and became what she later imagined for her own daughters—a wife and mother. Two of my sisters became nurses, and none is the teacher she thought I might be. Six of the seven daughters divorced. I was the first.

My main goal as a girl growing up with a bunch of sisters was to find time to be alone. On Sunday afternoons when the weather was nice, a favorite family activity was a car ride, often to a nursery to buy new plants for the yard. The rides usually ended with a stop for ice cream. As soon as Mom and Dad would let me stay home—I was probably about ten or so—I was willing to trade an ice cream cone for a few hours home alone. When I turned thirteen, Mom let me walk a half mile by myself to catch a bus that would take me to Portland. My first destination was the down-town library, where I loved to wander around, figuring out where things were and learning the card-filing system in the drawers of handsome wooden cabinets. I thrilled to the hushed stillness, the near-whispering voices of the librarians, the high ceilings and the broad stairway at the back. My other stop was Nordstrom, a few blocks away in the city center. Along with my interest in books, I was developing an interest in clothes. At that time girls were wearing white blouses with a Peter Pan collar on which you had your name embroidered. They looked nice under a sweater; my sister Judy had one, and I wanted one, too. Nordstrom was the go-to place for ordering the blouse with an embroidered name. Sometimes I met my best friend in town, or occasionally Becky went with me. My favorite downtown trips, however, were solo excursions. To this day I would rather shop alone than with others.

Judy and Mom often argued, and I wanted none of that. I had a few grievances—no shaving your legs until age sixteen, for instance. Instead of arguing, I feigned obedience, and eventually just shaved without saying anything. For the most part I was a good girl, got good grades, and caused no trouble. Once, while visiting Dad in a nursing home during his dwindling years, we talked about all the daughters. Judy was spoiled, he said. "We tried to do everything right and wound up making mistakes." Becky was Mom's helper, and so on through the list of younger sisters. What about me, Dad? "You," he said, seeming to think for a minute, "you just sort of raised yourself."

ITALY

1966–69

Passing through the military gate on the outskirts of Vicenza, we left behind the Italian countryside, the confusing signs and charming villages, for a familiar landscape of well-tended lawns surrounding one-story homes where majors and colonels lived. Villagio de la Pace looked like just another sprawling American suburb with curved streets. Our assigned home was at the far end of the development where the houses got smaller and then became two-story apartment complexes, four units per building. A second lieutenant is the lowest-ranking officer in the army, and we had housing to match. But for a young couple whose married life had begun less than a year earlier in a dumpy house shared with Ken's friends, this two-story, two-bedroom home seemed near perfect. Ours was a middle unit. Many other look-alike buildings—all of them painted white—were scattered along the back of Villagio de la Pace. Aside from the green lawns, other landscaping was minimal, with only an occasional splash of color in planter boxes at front doors. Many had swing sets and small bikes and trikes outside. All were orderly.

Ken opened the front door and carried Matt inside. I was right behind him, eager to assess the place that would be our home for the next three years. Army furnishings were adequate, but all in drab grays and tans. The carpet gave no hint of a pad underneath to soften the floor, and the rooms needed familiar items—lamps, pictures, keepsakes—that make a place feel like home. Ken and I had none of that. If you elope you don't have gifts to jumpstart your life together. It didn't matter to me at that moment; we could fix it up. What I remember most was how relieved I was to be there, away from the judgments and concerns of families back home.

Ken turned to me. "Well, this is it. What do you think?"

"We'll make this work," I said, not yet ready to fuss about all that it was not. I reached out to take Matt from Ken's arms, to hold him tight in our new home. "And what do you think, little guy? Does this look like home to you?" I carried him around the corner to the kitchen while Ken went upstairs to inspect the bedrooms and bathroom. "It seems barren," he said as he came down the steps. He was right, of course.

"Sure, but we can take care of that. I'll go shopping."

All the rest remained unspoken between us. Neither of us was a big talker. Reflecting on our relationship or feelings was not in our repertoire. Even today I can't imagine where discussion about our marriage might have gone. I saw him then as a pessimist to my optimist, laid back to my get-up-and-go. The reason I never imagined marriage during our college romance—it was mostly just the sex—was still with me. But now even the sex wasn't that interesting. What I hadn't yet discovered—or tried to—was Ken's basic goodness. What I saw then as stubbornness I know today as principled beliefs. Back then, I had what I thought were realistic, if unstated, expectations for our marriage: Enjoy our son together, be companions, and treat each other well. Romance was not in my equation.

I didn't yet know what it was like to be "in love," but I was pretty sure this was not it. Ken and I had an easy camaraderie, but, at least for me, nothing like the visceral connection I had read about in books and seen in movies. My best friend and college roommate had married her boyfriend in her junior year. They shared an interest in music and often sang together. Their happiness was so evident that they lit up the room even when they weren't singing. Whatever they had, it looked like love to me. The only other marriage I knew up close was my parents'. I saw them as partners—he made the money; she took care of the family. The only affection—if you can call it that—was Mom's routine nightly kiss on Dad's cheek or forehead. His reaction was a mumbled "g'night." Any romantic feelings I once had for Ken had been swept away in the trauma of a surprise pregnancy, a quick elopement, and the shame that followed. My only thought of a future had been getting to Italy and practice being married. Now, here we were.

Years later I convinced myself that I had never expected the marriage to last. But honestly, when I try to conjure what, if any, feelings I had during those Italy years, I can't come up with much. A graph of my emotional life during that period would be an even line with few highs and few lows. The occasional blip upward would reflect a trip or a time of peak enjoyment experiencing Matt's growth—crawling, then walking, and soon talking. What a little talker he was! There would be no downward dips. Ken and I did not experience great passion together, but neither did we argue.

We maintained. My aggravation with what I saw in him as stubbornness and my own unhappiness at home raising children would not emerge until after we collided with the realities of civilian life back in the United States.

My favorite feature of the new home was the small backyard, which looked out to a farmer's field beyond. Instead of being stuck in the middle of the complex, surrounded by other homes, I could gaze across the fence to the Italian countryside and occasionally watch the farmer on his tractor plowing his field—a daily reminder that a foreign country was at my doorstep, that there could be more to the next three years than toeing the line as a military wife.

It was 1966, and the traditions of army life were changing. Military wives were no longer expected to wear gloves at dressy affairs or leave calling cards at daytime social events, although some older career wives of majors and colonels still practiced those refined arts. As a low-ranking wife, I didn't get invited to many of those events in any case, which was a huge relief. Ken did not intend to remain in the army beyond his three-year stint, neither of us was interested in a busy social life, and I had never been one to make friends easily. I was friendly with a few close neighbors, women I could call for a cup of sugar, ask for recipes, and trade babysitting gigs.

I quickly realized, however, that I needed more in my new life than hanging around the house with a small child. After four intense college years, I wanted to continue learning and growing, and I saw no reason I couldn't do that while in Italy. One of our first purchases was a baby carriage, what Europeans call a pram. It was nothing like the strollers back home, which were low to the ground and designed for utility, not beauty. Our pram had large wheels on a frame that elevated it to waist high. It was dark blue, with a hood to shield its small passenger from the sun. With my short, dark hair and brown-eyed baby in a pram, I liked to think I might be mistaken for a Vicenza mom out for a stroll in the city square. It reminds me of how, as a girl, I yearned for independence within a family of seven girls. I've never been a joiner, and in Italy relished the notion, real or not, that I could wheel my baby through town without locals assuming I was a military wife.

Early in the first year I asked around about language teachers and was referred to Maria, an Italian woman who offered lessons in Vicenza. One warm day in early summer I headed to town with Matt in his pram to meet Maria. She was older than I, probably in her thirties, and attractive in a casual two-piece suit. We hit it off, and Maria is the one contact in Vicenza I remember, although we did not stay in touch after I left. I had studied Spanish for five years in high school and college, which was some help getting started, but it's embarrassing to admit now that I never mustered enough language skills to get beyond the basics; I had just enough to get by when shopping or traveling.

Ken and I must have been invited—or commanded?— to attend at least one important event, because I remember wanting a new dress and a haircut. I turned to Maria, who recommended both a salon and a dressmaker in Vicenza. Somehow the hair stylist was able to tame my unruly curls with a short, fashionable cut that made me feel even more like Italian moms in the town square.

The only dressmaker I had known was my mother, who used to sew dresses for me and my sisters. As a girl I enjoyed going to the fabric store with her to pick out a dress from a huge book of pictures and finding the pattern to match in the drawer filled with hundreds of envelopes filed by number. Inside were folded papers as thin as onion skin for the various pieces necessary to make the dress that matched the picture on the envelope. At home, Mom would pin those pieces of paper on the fabric we had selected, cut them out and sew them together. The one I remember best was a shapeless, drop-waist dress made of a floral cotton print on a buttery yellow background with three rows of brown rickrack around the bottom of the skirt. I wore it to my first day of high school in the fall of 1957.

Going to the Italian dressmaker in 1966 was nothing like any of that. Her shop in central Vicenza was in an old building dimly lit, with little natural light. Walls were lined with shelves full of fabric rolls; a long table was draped with a project in process. In the corner was a torso mannequin. Several rolling racks were filled with dresses, shirts, and jackets. The dressmaker was small, trim, and stylish with graying hair, friendly but businesslike. She knew just enough English and I knew just enough Italian to get down to the point. She understood when I said I was interested in "something dressy," and I understood her question: "Fantasiosa?"

"No, not fancy." I said. "Sophisticated."

"Ah, si," she replied.

And so it went. I selected a black silk fabric with a scattering of deep-red rosebuds. The fabric had a subtle sheen and felt like dark, smooth liquid as I draped it over my open palm. Under the light of a single bulb, the roses seemed to fade into the shadows of a black night sky. It was love at first sight—and touch.

"Ah, e molto elegante," she said approvingly.

We began a faltering conversation about the style.

"*Lunghezza pianale?*" she asked, gesturing to the floor.

"No," I said, "circa qui," pointing to my knees.

"Siete molto sottile," she said, moving her hands from my shoulders to my waist and outlining the shape of my hips. "Montare?"

"Si, si," I said, already imagining the simple, fitted dress she was suggesting for my slim figure.

She took my measurements and gestured about a zipper in the back, showing me a dress she had made with a perfect, nearly invisible zipper placket. "Buono," I nodded.

A week later I returned to try on the dress. It fit perfectly. It was the most beautiful dress I had ever worn, and I tried to tell her so.

"Grazie, grazie," I said. "Perfetto! Cosi bella!

I still remember the moment at the dressmaker's shop, looking into the mirror and seeing a sophisticated young woman in a beautiful dress and up-to-date hairstyle staring back at me. This was more than feeling Italian, this was about seeing myself as stylish and grown up for the first time in my life.

I don't recall the event where I wore it. Ken's reaction was "nice dress," but I knew the dress was *perfetto* and that I looked pretty darn good. It wasn't until years later, in Boise, after a divorce and—finally—finding what seemed like love, that I experienced what it means to have a man openly express his appreciation for not only my brains and companionship, but also how I looked in a fabulous new dress.

Ken and I thought of ourselves as lucky to be fighting the Vietnam War in Vicenza, Italy. Today that sounds flippant against the grim reality of the time. At least one high school classmate was killed in Vietnam, and a relative suffers to this day from his experiences there. That realization would come later, but at the time, we made the most of our good fortune as penniless newlyweds suddenly able to experience Italy and beyond. Venice was less than an hour's drive to the east; Verona, the beautiful city of *Romeo and Juliet*, was a mere half-hour to the west.

My first impression in all the cities and small hill towns we visited was how old everything was—buildings, hidden courtyards, statues, cobblestone streets and narrow alleys. History was ever present, a history that so predated the American story and had so many layers that I was constantly confronted by my own ignorance of a richer, deeper past than I had ever seriously contemplated.

Excursions in the region stand out for me, because so much of our life in Italy was as ordinary as the life of any young suburban couple. The only difference was that Ken walked out the door in his army uniform. An army base is like a small city where the basic needs of its residents are met. In Vicenza, Ken may have had an occasional training weekend, but his daily job was in the medical complex on base, practicing his new vision-care skills on military personnel and their dependents. I stayed at home most days, filling the hours with household chores—taking Matt for walks, making cookies, doing laundry and cleaning, reading during naptime—all the while fighting off boredom.

One early spring day a little over a year after our arrival in Italy, I went to the bathroom thinking my period had started. It was more than that, heavy and continuous, dark and clotted. I used one towel and then another to try to contain it. This was before *Our Bodies, Ourselves*, published in 1971 as a woman's guide to health and sexuality, and I was not well versed in how things worked "down there." But I soon realized this was not an ordinary heavy period, and called Ken, who was at work. I described the towels and what seemed to be clotted blood. He called the neighbor to look after Matt, then called for an ambulance. Ken arrived with the ambulance, and we sat side by side on a bench, saying little during the short ride to the hospital. I was embarrassed and beginning to feel lightheaded. Was this what Mom meant when she said she felt woozy?

At the army hospital, I was rushed onto a gurney, and the medical team began a series of blood transfusions. Once I had stabilized, the doctor told us that I had nearly waited too long. I had suffered a spontaneous miscarriage and lost a large volume of blood. I did not know I was pregnant and, at first, had assumed the heavy flow was because my period was a week or two late. At twenty-four years old, I felt once again like that naïve girl I used to be, and now also dangerously stupid.

A few days later Ken asked me how I felt about having been pregnant. Still dazed by the whole experience, I didn't have an answer. He persisted. "What if you hadn't miscarried?" he said. "How would you feel about having another baby?" We had not talked about a second child, but now Ken clearly was thinking about it. Our only shared pleasure was time with Matt. We thought, as most parents do, he was the most beautiful child ever, and smart, too. He was now an active toddler and already talking in whole sentences—subject, verb, object. "A little brother or sister? Maybe that's not such a bad idea," I said.

I now realize our thoughts about having another child did not focus on the future. Ken had grown up in Idaho and wanted to return there to start an optometry practice. Neither of us thought to explore that in any greater detail. Where would we live? How much could he make? Would I go to work? What about childcare? We were in the bubble of our right-now life—this home, stable army income, our love for Matt, opportunities to travel.

A few months later I was pregnant again. Everything was normal until, suddenly, it wasn't. I had just begun to wear loose-fitting maternity dresses and was feeling good. During a regularly scheduled appointment, the doctor spent more time than usual with a stethoscope listening to my slightly rounded belly.

"I'm not hearing what I want to hear," he said ominously. More tests followed, and we were told that the fetus was no longer alive. "These things happen," the doctor told us. "We don't really know why, but usually it means all was not right with the baby. Better it happens now than later."

I was scheduled for an induced "birth." It is oddly surreal to be on a maternity ward where other women are in labor with high expectations of greeting their new babies in the next hours, and all you are expected to do is deliver a damaged, lifeless fetus. After the first wave of disappointment, I faced the situation as a medical issue. I hadn't felt any movement, so the baby was not yet a reality to me, and I was doing what needed to be done. As with the pregnancy that had upended my life a few years earlier, I didn't develop an attachment to the life taking shape inside me. The baby I delivered, Matt, became real and precious to me only after he was born. As I entered the army hospital, I was more matter of fact than emotional. I was hooked up to a solution that would drip into my veins and induce labor within a few hours. When it was all over, I went home, glad to be done with it. No one asked if we wanted to know the gender (we didn't), and I don't recall ever being told what the problem was, only that there was no reason we could not—or should not—try again. We were young and healthy, and accepted that miscarriages, whether spontaneous or induced, happen for a good reason.

A year later, on September 4, 1968, Tim was born. Another healthy, beautiful, brown-eyed boy. This happy event, however, was not without a little preceding drama. Late in the pregnancy I tested positive for having had rubella, also known as German measles, the kind that can cause birth defects. I didn't remember any rash or illness during the pregnancy, so we did not know when I had it, but assumed it may have been associated with a recent episode of cold and sniffles. The later in the pregnancy, the narrower the odds of birth defects. But not knowing for certain was a worry. Defects associated with rubella can be serious, including eye problems, deafness, heart issues, and mental retardation. Since abortions were illegal in Italy, my only option for ending the pregnancy was to go to an army hospital in Germany. By now, I was emotionally invested in the pregnancy; I felt great, the baby was kicking, and I was looking forward to the change in routine a second child would bring into our lives. I also thought it would be good for Matt. Like me, Ken was from a big family (he had four siblings) and, continuing to ignore future realities, we couldn't imagine having an only child. After consultation with doctors, we bet on low odds of defects and decided to stay in Vicenza and continue with the pregnancy. (A year later, 1969, an antirubella vaccine was developed.) The day before Tim was born, Ken and I wheeled Matt in his pram through a fair in Vicenza. I remember it as a happy day, full of anticipation.

Ken and I settled easily into a two-child routine. He was a proud father and enjoyed time with his boys, handling everything from diapers to dinner. He took pleasure in photography, too, and had amassed a huge collection of photos of Matt. Now he began to capture Tim on film, along with family portraits of the four of us that we sent home to grandparents. Ken went to work every weekday, so he missed out on the frustrations of crying and whining children, and, for me, the occasional boredom that was a part of life at home with the kids day after day. I got out my sewing machine and made a few cute rompers for the boys. I didn't become interested in cooking until much later; in Italy I made a stab at some of the dinners I remembered from home—tuna-noodle casserole, spaghetti, hamburgers. A next-door neighbor was a more advanced cook, and she taught me to make beef stroganoff. My specialty as a teenager was chocolate chip cookies, so we had plenty of those. Ken was not picky about meals, and he didn't complain. He had learned to butcher meat while working at a shop in Pocatello where he was raised, and he always liked to survey the meat counter and select something to bring home. Since he usually cooked whatever he bought, those were my favorite meals.

We continued to see as much of Italy and Europe as possible. I particularly enjoyed seeing the walled hill towns of central Italy where, once again, the sense of history overwhelmed me as I contemplated those walls, built centuries ago to keep out invaders. Once we went with other military couples to view the wall that divided East and West Berlin, the physical manifestation of the Cold War that followed World War II. The wall had been built in August of 1961, only six years earlier, to prevent the people in communist East Berlin from escaping to the West. I stared at the fifteen-foot concrete barrier, speechless. It wasn't yet graffiti covered as it would become later; it was just a massive, stone-cold, gray edifice stretching far into the distance in both directions. Ken and I exchanged a glance and shook our heads in disbelief. Chilled by its ugly presence and purpose more than the cool weather, I pulled my jacket close and crossed my arms as a shiver ran through me. In contrast to other cities that impress with century upon century of history, here I witnessed a place of history in the making, a place where dangerous conflict seemed a real possibility. It wasn't until two decades later, while working in a newsroom at the time of the fall of the Berlin Wall, that I fully grasped the significance of those chilly moments at the base of the wall.

As if to punctuate the dangers haunting Europe at that time, soon the Cold War figured directly in the plans for our final trip before our scheduled departure from Italy in early 1969. Officers and their wives could fly, space-available, on a military plane to Greece, and many took advantage of that opportunity. Ken and I were finally successful in getting on a flight in the fall of 1968. We were excited to see the Greek Islands, the most exotic destination of our European stay. On August 20, 1968, Warsaw Pact troops, led by the USSR, invaded Czechoslovakia to crack down on a growing reformist movement in Prague. It caught the world by surprise, and U.S. planes operating out of bases in northern Italy had new orders. There would be no more flights to Greece for a Vicenza army officer and his wife.

While the Cold War was at our doorstep in Europe, a hot war of words raged back home. Opposition to the war in Vietnam, which had been gaining strength when we left early in 1966, continued to build throughout our three years in Italy, eventually converging with the civil-rights movement, women's liberation, student activism, and the free-speech movement. America was becoming polarized, but, while living abroad, I barely noticed. The journalist I had trained to become lay dormant. I was distracted by early motherhood, and at the time there was no CNN International—not even a daily newspaper or local television to crack through the tranquil barrier of Villagio de la Pace. I don't recall a single phone call to or from home. Mom occasionally sent *Time* magazine and wrote letters about the unrest, none of which penetrated her life in suburban Portland. But Mom and Dad were politically attuned liberals and fans of Wayne Morse, the Oregon senator who was one of the first politicians to speak out against the war, and so they became staunchly antiwar themselves. I read what Mom sent with great interest and shared it with Ken, whose political beliefs were close to mine, but not as firmly established, since he had grown up in a conservative Mormon family in southeast Idaho.

In mid-1968 I was shocked out of my relative complacency to learn of the killings of Martin Luther King Jr. in April and Robert Kennedy in June, and the chaos and confrontations at the Democratic National Convention in late August of that year. My once highly attuned political consciousness had been dulled by distance and circumstance. By then I was pregnant with Tim and unable to comprehend what was going on in the United States. It seemed as foreign to me as Italy had just a few years earlier. I began to look forward to returning and having access to current information, details, context—all that I was missing in the small world Ken and I had made for ourselves.

Once, during our last autumn in Italy, I came upon a rat in our laundry room, perhaps the downside of proximity to that farmer's field across the fence. I reacted with a ferocity I didn't know I had. Instantly thinking of my baby and little boy, I grabbed a broom, then a shoe, and somehow managed to corner that nasty beast and beat him to death. Yes, I really did *beat him to death*. I was proud of this newfound mothering instinct—however primitive—for protecting my children.

But even the best mother—and despite my victory over the rat, I knew I wasn't that—can't protect her children all the time. As I think about our departure from Europe, two incidents with the boys stand out. We had planned a short stay in London on our way home. While touring the London Tower, Matt, then about three and a half, bumped his head on a railing post and needed attention at the first-aid station. This only added to the edginess Ken and I were both feeling. We were leaving behind an easy life and heading into uncertainty. Ken had decided he would start a practice in Lewiston, Idaho, where a long-time optometrist was about to retire. I knew nothing about Lewiston, and traveling such a long distance with two small children had me somewhat frazzled, especially after Matt's mishap. We were flying to New York, where we would meet up with our car and drive across the country. I looked forward to the drive; it was New York, finding our car, and getting out of the city that concerned me. All that with an active little boy and an infant. Our Italy travels hadn't prepared me for this. At the same time, I was beginning to realize that as much as I loved the kids, the grind of motherhood, the self-abnegation, and the constant neediness of toddlers and infants drained me. Now I began to project that realization onto this place called Lewiston. Where would we live? What would I do there? How soon would Ken be able to make some money?

In the London airport awaiting our flight to New York, we found a booth in a grimy sandwich joint. Ken and Matt were on one side of the table, Ken helping Matt decide what he wanted to eat. Tim, a fussy, wiggly seven months old, was beside me. I propped him up against the wall while I looked at the menu. He was tired and wanted to lie down, not sit up. Next thing I knew he had slid off the slippery plastic bench seat and fallen to the filthy, sticky floor under the table. I scooped him up as he wailed and headed to our gate where I waited for Ken and Matt to join us for the long trip home.

For years I dreamed of small children dropping and falling out of my arms.

OHIO

1948

❧

D
ad had parked the shiny new trailer behind our
rented duplex in a leafy neighborhood of Ashland,
Ohio. My sisters and I were packed and ready to
go; we'd managed to smuggle our roller skates aboard the
trailer, Judy was her usual haughty self, ignoring her little
sisters. Becky and I could barely contain our excitement,
peering in every nook and cranny of the trailer and practicing how we would climb onto the dresser and then up to
the bunk at the front end. Finally, Mom shooed us outside.
"Okay, girls, that's enough. You're getting in the way here.
Go find Jenny." Two-year-old Jenny was a wild one. Judy
and Becky were supposed to be looking after her, but Jenny
on the run was hard to contain. Sometimes it took all three
big sisters—Judy, nine, Becky, six, and me—I was five—to
round her up.

The next day we would all climb into our blue-and-gray
Chevy Coupe, with the trailer already hitched up, and leave
behind all that I had ever known. A prized tricycle. The
kitchen counter I climbed on to reach the butter hidden
away in the top shelf of the cupboard; there, my fingers
made tracks in the soft yellow spread, and I sucked the

creamy richness into my mouth. The wide stairway where I fell and broke my collarbone. Until this day in the spring of 1948, that injury was the most exciting thing that had ever happened to me.

I was too young then to understand all that had transpired before that chaotic morning of anticipation. All I knew was that we were heading "west" where Dad had traveled recently and seen "the mountains." Mom and Dad warned us we would be cooped up in the car together for many days, and that we would sleep in the trailer. They promised interesting sights along the way—mountains, cities, deserts. I was ready for that. In the years since, I have always been open to the thrill of new and unknown places. I especially like car trips where the countryside unfolds for endless miles, as it did years later, after Italy, in the family drive from New York to the West Coast. This cross-country trek when I was a little girl was the beginning.

Our destination was Portland, Oregon, where Dad had gotten a job with a printing firm. He was a lithographer, one of those specialized craft jobs that has disappeared with the digital age. Dad's itinerary took us south and then west to Los Angeles, where we had relatives—and real beds to sleep in, and then north along the Pacific coast and over to Portland. After a few days on the road, we hit Route 66 and traveled through the Missouri Ozarks. By then we were getting stir crazy, so when Judy, our pack leader, suggested side trips for sightseeing, Becky and I always piped up in agreement, and lost; there was no time for side trips and no money for tourist traps. We had to settle for unusual sights such as oil derricks as we rolled through Oklahoma. That day we had noticed above-ground doors alongside farmhouses and learned they were entries to storm cellars. I had never heard of such a thing; the strange-looking doors and the idea of storm cellars were new concepts for me, an opening to the notion that traveling—especially by car—was filled with discovery.

"Tornado country," said Dad. Judy, who understood the term, described funnel clouds that tore down houses and trees. Nothing like the fear of a tornado to get little girls' imaginations going. What would the destruction look like? Feel like? Sound like? Late that day, Judy asked about some clouds in the distance. "Wrong time of year for tornados," Dad said. We were both relieved and disappointed. Seeing a real tornado—*that* would have been an adventure! That night the wind howled and rocked our trailer. Mom and Dad assured us all was well, and we fell asleep to the noise of wind gusts and rain pelting against the aluminum covering of our tiny home. The next morning Dad turned on the radio, and we learned that the first tornado of the season had passed within a few miles of where we were parked, doing considerable damage to towns on our route ahead. As we left Oklahoma City the next day, we saw debris, demolished buildings, broken trees, and, most alarming, smashed trailer homes—a sobering dose of reality for girls dreaming of adventure.

We were a few days beyond the Mississippi River and had yet to see our first mountain. Finally, in New Mexico, we saw a big bump on the horizon. "Is that a mountain?" Becky asked. Dad said it sure looked like a mountain. "What's it called?" asked Judy. In fact, it wasn't really a mountain. In the story Dad wrote years later about the family trek, he confessed that he tricked us. It was just a lofty hill that he and Mom decided to call Mount Tucumcari after the nearest town. At the time we didn't know any better and were satisfied; it meant we were closer to our destination.

Mom and Dad looked forward to visiting relatives in Los Angeles as a respite from days on the road and overnights with four squirrelly girls in a 150-square-foot trailer. One thing stands out about the visit: the Easter Morning Fire. My sisters and I were sleeping in a room that overlooked the garage when the grownups—minus Dad—rushed in. "Get out, get out quick. Hurry!" shouted Mom. The room was smoky. We were hustled out, but not before seeing smoke and flames billowing above the garage just outside our bedroom window. We knew our trailer was parked inches from that garage. Soon, the sirens blared. I remember exhilaration more than fear. My five-year-old mind didn't contemplate danger or even possible death to my father sleeping inside the trailer. All I knew at that moment was excitement.

Here's what happened: Dad and a nephew were sleeping in the trailer when they were awakened by a neighbor who saw the flames and banged on the door. Somehow, Dad, not a big guy, the nephew, who was younger and stronger, and the neighbor managed to pull the twenty-four-foot, two-ton trailer out of the driveway and across the street. The garage was a total loss. Tragedy averted and a new travel story to tell, we were on the road the next day. In the days and months that followed, I gradually realized the enormity of the Easter fire as I sensed the fear in my parents' voices as they retold the story.

For me, however, images of the blazing fire just beyond the room where I slept, the sound of the sirens, and Dad's harrowing tale of moving the trailer dissipated late in the sunny afternoon as we rounded a curve just beyond Ventura and saw the ocean. The sun sparkled off the breaking surf, and beyond it was ocean all the way to the horizon.

Nothing I had seen matched the grandeur of this sight. In the days ahead, the Golden Gate Bridge, the redwood forest, and mountains of northern California did not top that first ocean view on my list of Best Things I Saw on My Trip Out West. I couldn't know it at the time, but Oregon's ocean beaches, not the mountains that had inspired my father, would become the family connection, luring generations back to the beach, strengthening ties to our adopted state.

Despite the anticipation during the days-long drive north from Los Angeles, I have no visual memory of our arrival in Portland. We settled into a trailer park while Dad began his new job and devoted weekends with Mom to searching for a place to live. It would be weeks before the rain ended, the sky cleared, and we got our first glimpse of the iconic, picture-perfect shape of Mt. Hood looming over the city.

Our new two-bedroom rambler in a subdivision called Rose Garden Village was nothing like the two-story brick duplex we had left in Ohio, one of many older homes in an established neighborhood of similar one- and two-family homes surrounded by small yards and mature trees and shrubs. Rose Garden Village was a development southwest of Portland where the ground had been scraped of vegetation for new homes and roads. Our small house was made of concrete blocks painted a cream color. A covered walkway connected the house to a one-car garage. Dad said it was called a "breezeway." Two sets of bunkbeds were placed in one bedroom for me and my sisters. It was the first home Mom, then thirty, and Dad, thirty-two, owned.

I would learn later that the cost of building a home on a treasured rural lot back in Ohio was my parents' catalyst for moving. They called the lot Hickory Hill and drew up house plans. But when the estimate from the contractor came in at twelve thousand dollars, that dream was over, and a new one soon emerged. Within a few days they were shopping for a trailer. It was the postwar era, and we were among a wave of young families heading for the mountains to settle "out West."

At the new home, Mom and Dad got to work putting in a yard and planting flowers, including, of course, roses. Our little house became an icon of Portland's growing suburbs when it was featured in a local newspaper, including a photograph of four girls in nighties on their bunkbeds. Mom and Dad were proud of their house and family, and the newspaper clipping became a cherished keepsake. Only Becky was not pleased; she was embarrassed because in the photo her panties showed.

Soon we began the family exploration of the Oregon Coast. Less than two hours away from our home, the beaches—from Cannon Beach and Haystack Rock south to Lincoln City—became our frequent weekend playgrounds. We loaded up the car with shovels, buckets, beach towels, and a picnic lunch. "I see it, I see it!" I would shout from the back of the car. "No, you don't, that's just the sky," was the usual retort. After a day of shivering in the cold waves, hoping for the sun to emerge, and beachcombing with Mom and Dad, we'd pile back into the car—tired, sandy and often cranky—for the drive home.

I loved the different names and characteristics of the beaches: Hug Point, Arch Cape, Short Sands, Neahkahnie, Manzanita, Rockaway, Oceanside, Pacific City. We were especially attracted to beaches like the one at Arch Cape, a long stretch of sand that ended at a high cliff where waves broke over huge rocks near the shore. There we could spot sea urchins and starfish in the tide pools among the rocks, find driftwood along the high-tide line, and hunt for agates where waves washed in and scoured the beach. Gradually we stopped going to places without high cliffs and rocky shores. The long, straight stretch of Rockaway was too boring and dropped off our list, as did Pacific City, which was too far south and took too long to get to for a carload of little girls eager to have their toes in the sand. As the youngest sisters grew older, we loved Short Sands for the half-mile hike into a beautiful beach embraced by cliffs. After years of exploring, Arch Cape kept drawing us back. It has been a favorite, along with Oceanside farther south beyond Tillamook, for countless family reunions in the decades since those early forays.

As I write this, I realize my memories of the Oregon coast are not granular. They are elongated—a five-mile beach walk at low tide from Arch Cape to Cannon Beach, the trail at Ecola State Park with its overlook to a lighthouse, a hike on Cape Kiwanda with its expansive ocean views. So many deeply embedded memories of place and family braided through the generations, all thanks to a disappointment in Ohio and Dad's vision to move west.

Today, Arch Cape is as near to a family shrine as any place on earth. First Mom's ashes, in 1996, then Dad's in 2011, and then a brother-in-law's in 2016 were spilled among the rocks where Arch Cape Creek meets the ocean. My youngest sister, Susan—born in Oregon, after our earliest ventures to the coast—spoke for all of us at the family gathering to spread Dad's ashes. Sisters, spouses, children, and grandchildren formed a large circle on the sand near the breaking surf and the stream hugging the cliff. "Thank you, Dad, for bringing your family to Oregon and introducing us to its beaches," she said. Becky passed the bag of ashes. Each of us gathered a small handful and walked to the stream. Some tossed; I let the ashes fall slowly, watching as the water carried them through the rocks and into the ocean.

OREGON

1950–1965

⁂

Every two years in the six years after leaving Ohio, another sister arrived—Robin, Chris, and finally Susan. Even today it is not clear to me why Mom and Dad had so many children. Mom came from a family of nine and often said she had no intentions of having a large family. Judy and Becky and I speculated that they must have wanted a boy, but we never asked. Judy left home at nineteen, when Susan was three. We are all there in Judy's wedding pictures, but not until we became middle-aged and began to plan sisters-only retreats every few years are we together again—just the seven of us—in photos.

Despite sharing a cross-country trip in a trailer, bedrooms, and a love of the Oregon coast, the four oldest sisters were not especially close while growing up. Becky and I, nearest in age, played together when we were little, but as we outgrew paper dolls and playing office, our interests diverged. I was much more into climbing trees and exploring outside, while Becky was closer to Mom and spent more time inside with her.

We moved from Rose Garden Village after only two years, at the end of my first-grade year. Dad took a job as an officer of his union, which required a move to Kansas City, Missouri, where we were enchanted by the fireflies—we called them lightning bugs—but otherwise missed Portland. After two years, Dad made everybody happy by finding another job out West. Our house on Coleman Street in Cedar Mill, northwest of Portland, had been built with a separate living quarter in the daylight basement. Judy got to turn the kitchen into a bedroom—closet space instead of a refrigerator, desk instead of an oven and stove top, and of course her very own sink. Plus, all those drawers and cupboards for personal belongings. A private bedroom with special features was unheard of in our family. Becky and I shared the other lower level bedroom, and looked forward to the day we would have our turn in the kitchen bedroom.

Dad and Mom had lots of ideas for fixing up houses—inside and out. They finished the downstairs rec-room floor with black and white linoleum tiles, creating a large figure of a girl—designed with red squares angle-cut to form the shape of a skirt—in the center of the floor. It seemed a little goofy to me, but Dad and Mom were proud of the family icon on our playroom floor.

Both Mom and Dad read lots of books, and the living room coffee table was strewn with newspapers, *Newsweek,* and other magazines, always with a liberal bent. I remember Mom watching the Army-McCarthy hearings on television when I came home from school, occasionally registering her disgust: "Oh for goodness' sakes. That is just so wrong." But it was Dad I looked to for wisdom, true to the norm in that "Father Knows Best" era. One evening at the round table in our cramped eating space across the counter from the kitchen, Dad and Mom were discussing a trailer-home development proposed in the neighborhood, about a mile from our house.

"I hope it's not approved," Dad said, and Mom agreed. "I don't like the idea of that housing out here."

I was about thirteen, already showing signs of the opinion writer I would become, and piped up with a dissent: "But don't you think that kind of housing is needed? It's not that close to us, and you've said there's a shortage of housing for poor people."

"Well, I respect your thinking," Dad said, "but I just don't think it's a good project for that site." I don't know if it showed on my face, but I still remember the inner glow of satisfaction from Dad's stated "respect."

Still, that respect only went so far. When I was a senior in high school, Dad found a paperback copy of *Catch-22* on the kitchen counter and asked who was reading it. "Me," I said. "Why?" Dad was quiet for a moment, and then said, "I don't think that's an appropriate book for you." When I asked why again, he muttered something about language and all that military stuff. I didn't want to argue; I just wanted to read the book. Later I rescued it and hid it under my bed. From then on, I was careful not to leave books lying around the house.

Every family has its traditions; ours was Sunday-night supper and television in the downstairs playroom. The menu was always the same: grilled cheese or peanut butter sandwiches, fruit salad, and cocoa with marshmallows. One sister would be assigned to take sandwich orders; we had a choice of cheese—"yellow or stringy." Two or three of us would carry meals down the stairs from the main-floor kitchen, through the laundry room and into the playroom where we would settle in to watch television. Favorites over the years were *Hit Parade*, Ed Sullivan's variety show, and *Bonanza*.

While I fully participated in—and enjoyed—the family's Sunday dinners, the memory of wanting time to myself remains strong. Even today I savor the daytime silence of being home alone, no music, no NPR, just the domestic sounds of a house at work—the hum of the refrigerator, the dishwasher, clothes spinning in the dryer, the dog scratching at the door.

In my active stage as an adolescent, I would hit a tennis ball against the brick wall in the family room. Then I got hooked on baseball. I found some mitts and coaxed Dad into tossing a ball back and forth in the backyard for a half hour or so. Eventually we began to listen together to radio broadcasts of the Pacific Coast League's Portland Beavers. Radio is still my favorite way to enjoy a baseball game—the crack of the bat, the nervous energy of the crowd, and the announcers calling the plays. Dad even took me into Portland's Multnomah Field a few times to see the Beavers play. Late in his life Dad and I still enjoyed baseball, sharing the woes and rare joys of being a Seattle Mariners fan. Otherwise, Dad was very much a man of the fifties, titular head of the household who left most details—especially child rearing—to Mom.

Dad was an avid reader and did well in high school but didn't go to college. Years later I asked why. He told me he'd saved up a little money after high school and thought about college, "but there was also a nice little car I had my eye on." I asked him if he'd ever been sorry about buying the car instead of college. "Nope," he said with certainty and pride. "I think things have worked out pretty well for me without it."

In my years at Cedar Mill, I remember the family having a new car every two years, always a station wagon with maximum passenger space. After retirement, Dad spent his days in his garage workshop making scale-model cars of the early twenties and thirties out of fine hardwood. Dozens of those cars are now scattered in the homes of daughters and grandchildren, some treasured keepsakes, some collecting dust on forgotten shelves.

Mom and Dad were industrious people. Dad worked many overtime hours to earn extra money. Their homes were always nicely landscaped and well kept. All the daughters had chores, tasks that were posted on the refrigerator door. Saturday mornings we were supposed to help with house cleaning: our bedrooms, the utility room, and the recreation room. I didn't mind helping in the kitchen, but I hated Saturday cleaning. I wanted to be outside. Mom put me to work weeding flowerbeds, but that was as tiresome as cleaning house. By the time I was eleven I wanted a real job, something I could do for money.

We lived in Washington County not far from lush strawberry fields, and pickers were in demand, even pickers as young as eleven. Becky was agreeable, but first we had to get Mom's approval. One day near the end of the school year we headed up the stairs to ask Mom, who was in the kitchen preparing dinner. She turned around, wiped her hands on her apron and raised a questioning eyebrow as Becky and I stood there looking at each other. Finally, I spoke up: "Do you think it would be okay if Becky and I picked strawberries this summer?"

"Oh, gosh girls, are you sure you want to do that? Are you even old enough?"

"I saw it in the newspaper, Mom. We can do it."

Mom turned to Becky: "Do you really want to do this?"

"Yeah, I guess I'd like to try it."

Shortly after the school year ended, we were on the berry bus heading for the field. We were two nervous girls as we climbed off the bus at the field and were each handed a carrier—an oblong wooden box with sides about an inch and a half high, a wooden handle for carrying, and six one-pint cartons that fit inside. The field boss pointed out a row for each of us and where we could pick after we finished the row.

It was early June. The air was cool, and the rows were wet with dew. Before I began, I looked across the field to the acres of rows where other pickers were beginning, breathed in the fresh air, fragrant with the sweet smell of strawberries, and kneeled on the soft dirt. Soon I was under way, looking under the leaves of the plants to find the firm, ripe berries, pull them from their stems, and drop them into the first of the six empty cartons. It was not long before I realized I was moving down my row faster than my sister. I delivered my first full carrier to the field boss ahead of Becky and moved to a new row, having a good time, sometimes kneeling, sometimes standing and bending over. At the midmorning break, we ate the snack we had packed at home. Becky didn't have much to say, but I could tell she thought this was a drag. Pickers on the bus going home at noon were rowdy compared to those on the sleepy early-morning ride. Many of them had picked together before, and the bus was abuzz with conversation, joking, tossing of berries, and singing "99 Bottles of Beer on the Wall." We went back the next day, finished the short season, and moved into bean fields later in the summer. For reasons I could not understand, Becky liked picking beans better than strawberries. Not me—the field didn't smell good, the midsummer air was heavy, and the slimy feel of a rotting bean nearly made me gag. The next summer, Becky gave up working in the fields, but I returned to strawberry picking two more summers. I was outside, I made a little money, and I realized that I liked to work.

Unfortunately, I hated my next job.

I was happy to be hired by Rogers Five and Dime in nearby Cedar Hills, where I had a more grown-up job than picking strawberries, but I never figured out exactly what I was supposed to do. "Work the floor," the boss said. Too shy to ask for details, I roamed the aisles of cheap toys, sewing notions, small kitchen gadgets, soaps, and perfumes, assuming I would figure out in a few days what I was supposed to do there. Customers did not flock to Rogers, and those who showed up didn't need help from "the floor girl." I wandered around, straightening up merchandise that didn't need it, and found refuge in the only available reading, the card aisle, where I pretended to sort greeting cards. In my summer of work there I occasionally found something out of order and felt modestly useful. But, really, how interesting can birthday and sympathy cards be day after day?

I also had many babysitting jobs, including one that combined daytime childcare and household help. I liked the evening babysitting jobs best, because I didn't have to spend too much time taking care of kids. After their bedtime, I could read or watch television and eat ice cream.

It wasn't until later when I was a college journalism student and got a summer job at the Hillsboro *Argus* that I discovered satisfying grown-up work. I wrote obituaries, translated wedding forms into stories, and wrote features, including one about taking a flying lesson at the local airfield. Hardly high-falutin' journalism, but it was everything I wanted from a job—interesting, challenging, busy, and fun.

From the discovery as a five-year-old that I could read, I loved going to school. In fourth grade at Cedar Mill Elementary I also liked recess and looked forward to playing dodge ball—we called it "prison ball" back then—and to Friday spelling bees. I was a good speller. Fifth grade is about the time girls start noticing boys as something other than a dodge ball target. I was slow to come around to that, but prodded by friends asking, "Who do you like?" I tried to come up with an answer. One day after giggling with girlfriends during the lunch break, I wrote an I-like-you note and snuck it to Alan, who sat behind me. I felt brave, especially when Alan told me after school that he liked my note. Still, it wasn't as much fun as dodge ball. Once, in sixth or seventh grade, I went to a party where we played Spin the Bottle. I sat in a circle with the others, dreading the possibility of the bottle pointing at me. I was not interested in going into a back room for kissing or even handholding. Passing notes was as far as I would go. I retreated into a shyness that came naturally to me, avoiding Spin-the-Bottle-type parties, and becoming the quiet girl who gets good grades.

Having bypassed the giddy boy-girl business of adolescence, I entered high school devoid of girlish charms, serious rather than flirtatious. I usually had one or two close girlfriends and hung out on the fringes of the "popular" girls but didn't feel like one of them. Nevertheless, for reasons that to this day befuddle me, I tried out for the freshman cheerleading squad. Maybe someone suggested I should, and I was flattered by that. Perhaps I thought it would get me into the "in" crowd. Or maybe I simply liked the idea of the vigorous activity. I was selected and soon realized I wasn't any good as a cheerleader; rhythm and timing often eluded me. I did love the skirts, however. We were the Sunset High Apollos, and our colors were purple and white. In the style of the day, our knee-length skirts had sharp-edged pleats, fitted white from the waist to the hips where the pleats flared out with purple inside, creating a kicky mix of purple and white stripes.

At the end of the year all six cheerleaders were up for election for the next year. Why I didn't quit outright after the first year is as big a mystery as why I tried out in the first place. Alas, I was the only one of the original squad of six to lose the election. I'm sure I must have been a tiny bit relieved that I didn't have to get out in front of high-school sports fans anymore, but the only thing about this whole cheerleading episode I *do* remember, besides the cool skirts, is how crushed I was by losing. The only one! I was so embarrassed I wanted to hide out for days. Later, I would experience something similar, only far more intense: A deep sense of failure and shame upon learning I was pregnant.

After my failure as a cheerleader I concentrated on doing what came more naturally—studying and getting involved in what I saw as less frivolous student activities, such as student government and working on the high school newspaper, the *Scroll*. The newspaper idea came after my English teacher, Shirley Malcolm, singled me out in front of the class for a writing assignment I had turned in. I still remember her words: "Mindy is a writer; she writes with style." I wasn't sure what she meant, but I took it to heart.

My first date in high school was another failure. His name was Chris; he was a guy I knew from church, Bethel Congregational in Beaverton. He was a year older, quiet; the kind of boy mothers liked a lot for maturity, intelligence, and kindness. He also had a bad case of acne. When he asked me out, I said yes, thinking I had to start somewhere, and he seemed nice enough. All I remember about this date is silence, not where we went or what we did, only that Chris was driving and I sat beside him, closer to the door than to him. I remember a futile mental search for something—*anything*—to talk about, words to fill the embarrassing silence that surrounded us. My mind was blank. Chris must have been equally shy, probably thinking the same thing, because he wasn't talking either. It was our first and last date.

I dated a few other boys I knew from high school and realized that having high school in common at least provided fodder for conversation. One boy later became the steady beau of my best friend. They went off to college together and eventually married. Another classmate was Skip, who a few years later would give me the love letter and a 45rpm record of a song he'd written about me. We were an item off and on through high school, but—much to his dismay, I suspect—I graduated never having been kissed, despite some cheek-to-cheek dancing to "Moon River" at a school dance.

———

COLLEGE WAS A DO-IT-YOURSELF PROJECT FOR ME. My sister Judy had taken off for California to find work after high school and was soon married. Becky was in nursing school, dating the guy she would eventually marry. Mom and Dad thought college would be a fine thing for me but had little money and even less knowledge of how to make it happen. "Maybe you could apply for some scholarships," suggested Mom. It was 1961, and they were proud of what they had achieved in life without college educations. They didn't imagine a world in which women—their daughters, no less—would pursue college degrees and have careers outside the home.

A high-school teacher was my college guide. Just a few years out of college herself, Ginny Cooper, advisor of the *Scroll*, was an enthusiastic mentor. We had become close while working together on the newspaper.

I was serious about high school journalism, tackling school budgets and other "hard news." Reporter's notebook in hand, I went to a few school board meetings and into the principal's office to interview him about changes in attendance policy. Reporting became the ideal outlet for my natural curiosity about the world around me. What I liked most was making sense of the complex and writing readable stories.

One February day in 1961, the latter half of my senior year, after the *Scroll* deadline had passed and the busy newsroom had cleared out, Mrs. Cooper pulled me aside and asked what my plans were after high school. I didn't have an answer. Most of my friends were going to the University of Oregon or Oregon State, but I didn't want to go to a big school. The truth was I had seen some brochures of small colleges and dreamed of going to a place like one of those. Pomona was the one that stuck in my mind, but I knew it was financially impossible, so I didn't mention it to Mrs. Cooper.

"Have you thought about Pacific?" she asked.

"Oh, maybe a little," I said. I knew that was where she had gone and didn't want to be dismissive, but after high school I hoped to be farther away from home, not in Forest Grove, a small town a mere half-hour drive down the road.

"I've talked to Professor Rowe about you. He thinks you should consider it, and so do I."

Ginny had remained in touch with Cliff Rowe, the journalism professor, after she graduated. Rowe worked summers as vacation relief on the copy desk for Portland newspapers, had contacts at newspapers throughout the Northwest, and liked to tout his record of sending graduates off to newspaper jobs.

I was surprised that she had talked to the professor and flattered by his apparent interest, but I knew that money was an issue. "Thanks, that's really nice, but I don't think my family can afford it."

"Let's sit for a minute," Ginny said, pulling out a chair for me along the *Scroll* paste-up table. She told me that Professor Rowe was sponsoring a newswriting competition for interested high school seniors in the region. The stakes were high: The winner got free tuition for the *last two years* if you enrolled at Pacific.

"He wants you to enter," she said, explaining all I'd need to do was spend a day on campus and write stories based on facts presented to all the contestants.

Well, I didn't ace it; I came in second. I've forgotten the details of the stories I wrote; all I remember is two scenarios, one for a feature story, the other for a news item. Basic stuff. Luckily for me, the first-place student didn't want to go to Pacific, and I was offered the scholarship. Combining my negligible savings, several small, local scholarships, a few hundred dollars from Mom and Dad, and work-study jobs provided by Pacific, the impossible became possible, and I enrolled.

IDAHO

1969–1970

⸻

L ewiston sits in a deep canyon at the confluence of the Clearwater and Snake rivers in north central Idaho. When Ken and I and the boys arrived in 1969, the rivers ran free, but not for long. Lower Granite Dam, the last of four dams on the Snake before it meets the Columbia, was completed a few years later, after we had left, and brought slack water—essentially a reservoir—to Lewiston and Clarkston, its twin city across the river in Washington State.

All of that—the flowing rivers, the controversy over the soon-to-be reservoir—was lost on me as I faced the transition from a stable income and military housing to an unknown future. My first impression of Lewiston was that the rivers were nice, but the town stank—literally. A huge paper mill on the east end of town spewed out smoke and fumes that smelled like rotten eggs. It wasn't too bad downtown, and seldom was detectable around the river bend in the neighborhoods up the hill south of town where we found an apartment to rent. Financial realities hit almost immediately. Ken quickly discovered that the optometry practice he was taking over from a retiree was not a thriving business. Ken was serious about optometry and intent on running the practice his way. I didn't understand the nuances of "his way" versus other ways, but it seemed to me he wasn't listening to his clients or reaching out to other optometrists for advice. Early on I tried to talk to him about it, but he was dismissive. "You just don't understand," he would say. He was right, of course. I didn't understand, but at the time I experienced it as a stubborn contrariness in Ken that I hadn't noticed before. I chalked it up to stress.

And I was dealing with my own stress. Soon, it became obvious we couldn't afford the first apartment, and we began looking for something cheaper. A rundown furnished house set back from the sidewalk on a big lot in the same neighborhood seemed acceptable. There was room for the kids to play outside and trees to shade us from the hot summer sun. At less than eight hundred feet of elevation, Lewiston is the lowest spot in the state and often the hottest. The house itself left a lot to be desired. It had several do-it-yourself add-ons, a low ceiling, bad lighting, and inadequate insulation. We suffered in the summer heat and used space heaters to keep warm in cooler weather. Once, I smelled something burning and found one of Tim's many stuffed animals against the heater—singed but not yet ruined. It was nap time, and he had probably tossed it before falling asleep.

"We've got to get out of this dump," I told Ken that night. "I'm going to the newspaper to see about a job so we can afford something decent."

"What about the kids?" he said.

"Maybe I can work evenings while you're home." I had no idea if that was possible; I was just determined to try to change our circumstances.

The *Lewiston Morning Tribune* was one of the best things about Lewiston. It was a newspaper with a long history, founded in 1892, and owned by a local family who cared deeply about local, independent journalism. The newspaper was well regarded across the state. I didn't know any of that when I walked through the door late one afternoon to ask about a part-time job. I didn't even have a resume. The crowded newsroom was noisy with activity. A few reporters were on the phone, others milled about, and two were shouting at each other across the room. In the far corner a teletype machine made a constant clatter as it spit out yellow tape from the Associated Press. I spoke to the woman at the front desk, who summoned the editor. He looked my way, smiled, and walked over. I quickly spilled out my story. He asked a few questions and hired me on the spot: "We can find some things for you to do in the evening and see how it goes from there." The editor introduced me to a few people in the newsroom. The *Tribune* staff then had several writers with checkered pasts, including one sweet older fellow who I later learned had served time in prison for being an accomplice to a killing. He drove the getaway car. The *Tribune* didn't hire people so much as collect them. An untested novice, I was happy to be added to the collection as a roving reporter in the evenings while Ken was home with the kids.

My assignments were not exciting, but my stories got in the paper, including a report on a musical event in Clarkston. I don't know anything about music, but I treated it like a "review"—naming a few of the pieces, describing some aspect of the music and the audience reaction. One of the editors referred to these stories as "a represent"—representing the interests of readers, regardless of news value, to show respect for them. Occasionally, I was sent to a night meeting or public hearing that was more substantive than a represent and demonstrated that I could also deliver an understandable news story. I knew about the inverted pyramid and how to capture and include pertinent quotes, getting names in the story. I didn't care what the assignment was; I just loved being in the newsroom. I liked the irony, sarcasm, high spirits of the reporters and editors, the dusty smell of the paper we typed our stories on, and the intoxicating fumes of the glue we pulled out of a bottle on a brush to paste our pages together. The editor liked to hold the pages up and, if his hand was over his head and the pasted pages reached the floor, he was pretty sure the story was too long. I was hooked.

I remember the day Cecil Andrus, then a candidate for governor of Idaho, came to the *Tribune's* offices. He was on a campaign swing through north Idaho, and the *Tribune* where the liberal editors were staunch supporters made for a congenial stop. As I would later discover, Andrus was a gifted politician who seemed to be a friend to everyone he met. He knew most of the *Tribune* staff, but he soon spotted me as a newcomer and made a special effort (or it seemed that way to me at the time) to chat with me. I fell under his spell, as did much of Idaho. He won the 1970 election and eventually served fourteen years as governor. Meeting the state's leading politician further fixed in me the notion that I belonged in a newsroom.

The hours I spent working at the *Tribune* lifted my spirits and mitigated the hours spent cleaning house, shopping for groceries, cooking, and taking care of two active little boys. Ken seemed content to spend evenings at home and make supper for Matt and Tim. While the little extra money I made helped, Ken still worried about his business. I would come home from work eager to tell Ken about my assignment, only to find him asleep with the kids. After a few weeks at the *Tribune,* it was clear the job would last, and we were able to move to a more suitable house, farther up the hill away from town. It was a nice-looking yellow house, very small, but light filled. Two tiny bedrooms, a bathroom, cramped kitchen, and front room with a table at one end was just big enough for the four of us. The job and the move reduced my stress. I began to enjoy reading to Matt and Tim, getting down on the floor to play with them and taking short walks to the park. A big help for me—and many other young mothers—was the premiere of *Sesame Street* in November of 1969. That splendid mix of characters—real people and Muppets, music, and stories—was a lifesaver, something Matt and I could enjoy together, and, when he was a little older, Tim, too.

Having a television also made it easy to once again pay attention to what was going on in the world. One afternoon shortly after moving into the yellow house, I watched Neil Armstrong's moon landing while ironing clothes in the front room. I remember feeling proud, proud to have supported President Kennedy who inspired the moon mission. I know those sentiments seem corny in today's more cynical age, but the memory of standing by that ironing board enthralled by the moon landing on the small screen remains vivid. Less than a year after the moon walk—May of 1970—pride turned to horror with news from Kent State in Ohio, where the National Guard had opened fire at an antiwar protest. Four students were killed, and more than a dozen others injured. The easy years in Villagio de la Pace seemed far away and long ago. And I was once again engaged—intellectually and emotionally—in American political life.

About this same time, Ken began looking for another optometry position. He had nearly given up on Lewiston when he learned of another possibility. We were seated at the small table after dinner one night when he surprised me with a question: "What would you think of Boise?" Now that we had the house and I was working, I was settling into Lewiston, not ready for another change so soon, and slow to respond. "Do you think you've given it enough time?"

Despite my initial reluctance, the notion of moving to Boise, the state capital, gradually became appealing. I've always been open to change, and within a few weeks I began to think of possibilities at the *Idaho Statesman,* the state's largest newspaper. By then, I was aware of the *Tribune's* statewide reputation, and had a hunch that my experience there, along with a reference from the editor, would give me a good shot at a job with the Boise paper. I wasn't yet aware of the burgeoning feminist movement, but my optimism about getting a job in Boise surely bubbled up from a not yet acknowledged sense that I was an outlier, a competent, ambitious young woman in a man's world. My hunch proved correct.

As I came around to the move, however, I didn't want to jump into something that might not work out for Ken. I wondered whether he could work successfully with another optometrist. I knew that one of the reasons he became an optometrist was to be his own boss, to not answer to anyone else, to do things his way. And his way, as I began to understand, was to emphasize visual training along with the more routine practice of prescribing glasses. Many clients at that time were resistant to vision training, and that frustrated him. He was somewhat of an outlier in the optometry field then, but—as I would later realize—ahead of his time. He was also stubborn by nature. I did not share my concerns with him; it seemed his decision was firm.

BOISE

1970–74

A s Ken and I headed for Boise, 270 miles south of Lewiston, I was filled with hope fueled at least partly by the geography. We left a town wedged deep in a cleft gouged by two rivers, driving south past the stench of the paper mill and uphill through a narrow canyon that opened upon a vast prairie surrounded in the distance by white-capped mountain peaks. We were still hundreds of miles from Boise, but to me this high, open landscape, the fresh, grassy smell of the fields, and the start of a new decade promised a change for the better.

Idaho is a long state, nearly six hundred miles from top to bottom. It's skinny in the north—barely sixty miles across in the Panhandle, tucked between Washington State and Montana—but begins to fatten in the center and then widen in the south, where the fertile Snake River plain runs from Wyoming for over three hundred miles to Oregon in the west. The middle of the state is a mostly inaccessible crush of mountains, which includes the largest contiguous area of protected wilderness in the United States. Americans know Idaho—if they know it at all as distinct from Iowa— for its potatoes. But for most residents the Idaho spud is a meaningless symbol, especially in northern and central Idaho, where mountains, forests, lakes, and rivers are the authentic symbols of the state.

Farther south the mountains give way to lava flows and finally to the river valleys and high deserts of the broad southern portion of the state. Boise sits at an elevation of two thousand seven hundred feet, where the desert, bisected by the green Boise River valley, meets the Rocky Mountain foothills, known locally as the Boise Front.

I thrilled at the sights as we drove south, excited that we had left behind a hard year, but I couldn't read Ken's silence. Was he nervous about this fresh start? Or still disappointed about his inability to get a solo practice going in Lewiston? Matt was now an easygoing five-year-old; Tim a two-year-old toddler who ran the emotional gauntlet between sweet and stubborn. The predictable life we had known for three years in Villagio de la Pace was in the distant past. I see now how ill-prepared we were for a life of struggle—scrambling to earn a living, enduring grim searches for housing, and a marriage that felt like two people going through the motions. Somehow, we maintained a steady calmness—no fights or arguments, but also few romantic gestures. I'd turn away in bed when he reached out. We managed a family life, but lacked the warmth and energy of a close, intimate relationship.

I looked forward to new opportunities in Boise, but starting all over was another financial hurdle. Again, we settled for less-than-adequate but affordable housing—an apartment near two busy roads. I told myself it was just temporary; soon we'd find a nice little house.

One day, before we found that nice little house, I stood in the tiny kitchen starting dinner for the boys, exhausted, stewing over my coming night shift news job, when Tim began hollering. At the *Idaho Statesman,* my first assignment was covering the cop beat. I began at six and quit at midnight. I hated the job and the hours, but we needed the money, and it was my entree to the *Statesman.* Not only did I dislike the night cops assignment, I wasn't very good at it. The officers were patronizing— "jerks," I thought to myself. I was the first "girl" doing the job—and I dreaded the possibility that a serious crime or fire would happen on my watch. I wanted to cover people and policy, not crime and fires.

I stepped out of the kitchen to see what the ruckus was all about. The boys sat on the floor of the small living room, a pile of wooden blocks and Matchbox cars all around.

"Matt, what's going on here?"

"Nothin', Mom. I didn't do anything. He just started crying."

Tim was not yet able to talk much, but made himself clear by pointing an accusing finger at Matt. I picked him up and looked at the blocks. "Were you building something special?"

"Uh uh," he said, between sobs.

"Did Matt knock over your blocks?"

He nodded his head and pointed his finger again. "Bad Matt!"

I looked at Matt, cocked my head: "Why?"

"He was messing with my cars. Why is it always my fault?" He scrambled to his feet, stood defiantly with his legs far apart, and glared at Tim. "I *hate* him!"

Without thinking, I reached out and slapped him. Matt was wide-eyed with surprise. I stood still for an instant, shocked by what I'd done. Tim howled as I put him down and gathered Matt in my arms, overwhelmed by a wave of remorse.

"Oh, sweetheart, I am so sorry. I promise I will never do that again."

Years later I remembered a long-ago moment when I'd witnessed Mom slap Judy. I recalled the surprise and unease I felt. Small, singular moments in the lives of two mothers and two children. Something snaps inside, and you realize a capacity to act out in a way that is wrong, so very wrong.

The stint on the night cops beat at the *Statesman* didn't last long. I was promoted to a daytime news beat and soon began covering city and county government, a meaty assignment that felt like just the right fit. It was the early seventies, and the Nixon administration was sending federal money to cities to remake themselves in the name of "urban renewal." In Boise, acres of a rundown area near the city center, including a small Chinatown, had been flattened and paved for temporary parking lots intended to become a downtown shopping center. This was a controversial story I could dig into. Even better was the emergence of a long-running effort to create a greenbelt along the Boise River. When I asked the city editor if I could work on that story, he said yes. I felt like an established reporter with a growing reputation inside the newsroom and out on the beat.

Ken got off to an okay start with his optometry practice, and we settled into a small house near his office to begin our life in Boise. In our life together we existed only as parents, enjoying family time as we discovered the city, its river, the high desert to the south, and the nearby mountains. We still had not developed a habit of discussing our marriage, our feelings, or the future. The move to Boise didn't change that.

"Who wants to learn to fish?" Ken said one night after dinner.

"Me! I do, I do," said Matt.

Tim piped up. "Me, too. I wanna fish."

We made plans for the following Saturday. "But I don't want to learn to fish," I told the boys. "Can I read a book while Dad teaches *you* guys to fish?" I gave Ken a you-know-what's-coming glance.

Ken knew I didn't share his passion for fishing, and I'd told him that when he thought the boys were old enough, it was up to him to do all the rigamarole—messing with gear, baiting the hook, unraveling snags, gutting the fish. I had never experienced the thrill of catching a fish, and all the rest of it didn't seem worth the effort. I didn't intend to start now, dealing with the kids while Ken moseyed on down the stream, out of sight.

Saturday morning, we headed for a stream far enough from town to have some space to ourselves. We found the spot Ken had in mind: a grassy bank for me, trees a safe distance from snagging a wayward cast by a small boy, and a clear stream flowing around rocks and logs that offered hiding places for wary trout. Perfect. Soon three heads were bent down over hooks and worms, rods and reels. Ken made the first cast of the small rods, and the boys had big smiles as they grabbed hold and waited for the first bite. I opened my book.

The fish did not cooperate, and soon the small platoon moved downstream. My peace and quiet lasted for less than a short chapter. I looked up to see the trio approaching. "I don't like fishing," said Tim.

"Sorry," said Ken, smiling and shrugging his shoulders.

"That's okay. Tim and I will do some exploring." It was a beautiful day and I was content to be out in the cool, fresh air filled with sounds of swaying trees and water lapping over rocks. The book was mostly an excuse to have Ken take charge of the fishing. Being out-of-doors was the main goal, and I always carried a book along, just in case.

Ken and Matt turned to head back down the stream as Tim and I went to the water's edge in search of bugs, and rocks to throw upstream. Matt and Ken soon returned to show me a small, undersized fish that Ken quickly returned to the water. Matt was finished, too. I spent an hour or so exploring the streamside bank with the boys, until Ken returned with two pan-sized trout. "Dinner," he said with a grin.

Today when I muse about the Boise years and why the marriage lasted as long as it did, I recall days like that on the stream. There were others: A spring day in the desert abloom with wildflowers, tubing the Boise River on a hot summer afternoon, family time at Camel's Back Park near our house. All this lent a pleasant veneer of togetherness to a household where my private discontent was growing— where it was becoming clear I'd have to continue setting books aside.

I grew to love Boise, a vibrant, growing city of seventy-five thousand. A newspaper reporter's job is to talk to lots of people, learn the ins and outs of local politics, and write about the most interesting happenings in the life of a city. I had always been curious about the world around me, and being a journalist is a license to be nosey. Just as in high school when the role offered a path outside my shy-girl shell, now the newsroom was an escape from the domestic confines of being a wife and mother.

AN INTRIGUING STORY OF THE ERA WAS THE EMERGENCE

Mindy Cameron

of the women's movement. I didn't write about it; I lived it. Women had been organizing around the country since the late sixties, when I was a young mother in Italy, oblivious to the cultural undercurrents overwhelming my contemporaries back home. The struggles Ken and I had getting restarted in Idaho continued to blur all but the major events in the outside world. By the middle of 1971, finally settled in Boise, I could begin again to look beyond myself and sense the changes underway. Through contacts I made as a reporter, I learned of a group of women starting a consciousness-raising group. "Would you like to attend?" an acquaintance asked. I didn't hesitate.

I was uncertain what to expect as I walked into the meeting place at the Boise Cascade headquarters, the workplace of one of the group leaders, a former journalist then working in corporate communications. About twenty women were gathered, seated on comfortable sofas and easy chairs. I grew more at ease as, one by one, we introduced ourselves. These were intelligent and interesting women—a mix of professionals and community volunteer leaders, not a radical in the bunch. We didn't plan marches or demonstrations, only shared our experiences and concerns to support each other in our male-dominated environments. Women were doing the same thing in living rooms, church basements, and offices across the country. Some radicalized, but most of us just grew a little wiser and more confident, gradually seeing the world—and ourselves—from a different slant.

Soon I began reading *Ms.* magazine, which first published in January of 1972. *Ms.* had a feature called "CLICK," a story highlighting the moment a woman discovered she was being discriminated against. My own CLICK moment came one day at work. Physically, newsrooms haven't changed much over the years. They remain large open spaces filled with individual desks. Usually glass-enclosed offices of top editors line the walls, giving those editors a view to the scattered desks of reporters and to the center cluster of copy editors, the final stop where grammar is corrected, commas inserted or deleted, and, most important, headlines are written.

My desk was in the news section of the *Statesman*. As a government reporter I was a novelty in the newsroom, the first female to cover anything considered hard news—as opposed to "soft"—at the paper. The few other women on the staff wrote features in the women's section.

I sat next to the business reporter, Steve. One day I learned that Steve, who had experience similar to mine, was making ten dollars more a week than I was. In those days, ten dollars would buy a whole bag of groceries—or more. I went to the office of the managing editor and knocked on the closed door. He was a very formal man, not the kind of editor who walked around the newsroom and chatted or asked about what you were working on. He wore a shirt and tie, and everyone always addressed him as Mister.

"Mr. Hronek," I said, "do you have a minute?"

"Yes, of course," and he pointed to a chair, even though he continued to look at the open newspaper on his desk.

I got right to the point. "I'm wondering about a salary discrepancy."

He raised his head from the newspaper and looked directly at me. "What are you talking about?"

"Well, I found out that Steve makes ten dollars more a week than I do, and I know he doesn't have any more experience. I'm wondering why we aren't paid the same amount."

A long pause. "I can explain that," he said slowly. "Steve has a family to support."

CLICK! The instant I realized that being a woman was an excuse for a lower paycheck was the moment I became a feminist. I didn't explain to Mr. Hronek that I was the major wage earner in my family while my husband was building his optometry practice, which was going more slowly than anticipated. I didn't think it would be fair to Ken to disclose that, and I didn't think I would get anywhere with Mr. Hronek. Instead, I said nothing, just sat there in silence for a few seconds, then got up and left the office. I quietly closed the door behind me as the editor returned to his newspaper.

WHILE KEN AND I BOTH HAD OUR CHALLENGES AT WORK, our social lives were active and rewarding. Despite our personal distance, we made friends among a small circle of the city's young progressives who were pushing back against urban renewal, working to create the greenbelt, and trying to stop dams and save the White Cloud and Sawtooth mountains in Idaho's wild center from new mining incursions. Through his interest in preserving pristine waters for fishing, Ken became involved with other like-minded friends who formed the Idaho Conservation League. It exists today as the premiere environmental organization of Idaho.

After a few years I was assigned to the state government beat. The governor's office was a regular stop, and on a few occasions Governor Andrus and I reminisced about Lewiston and the *Tribune*. Covering the state legislature was a grind and rarely yielded a memorable story. Maybe that's why my most vivid memory is the bottle of scotch the *Statesman's* political editor stored in the bottom drawer of his desk in the fourth-floor suite of press offices in the Capitol. He never offered me any, but later I decided if I was going to drink what the top dogs drank, I'd choose scotch.

Occasionally I attended evening events related to journalism or politics without Ken. News people are a noisy, talkative crowd; they are in the know and gossip about inside stuff. For the first time in my life I felt like an insider, and I loved that scene. Ken said he was not comfortable in larger settings that included many journalists and elected officials where I knew many more people than he did. At the time I thought he seemed happy to stay home with the kids, but now I wonder if he really was, or if I was just taking advantage of him and his reticence.

One night after an event, a prominent man in the community offered me a ride home. Stopped in front of my house, he put his arm around my shoulders, told me how great I looked, and tried to pull me close. I resisted, got out of the car, and went into my house.

Another time a well-loved community elder, who knew everybody and everything and respected journalists as much as we respected him, offered me a ride in his taxi and made a move on me. Shocked, I nonetheless excused the episode as a drunken mistake—by him, not me. But his actions eroded my respect for him.

Consciousness-raising sessions, *Ms.* magazine, and my earlier limited dating life had not prepared me for this, and I was at a loss for how to respond. In both instances I pushed away. The encounters were such surprises I had no smart verbal retort. I was not interested in these men—both were married and knew that I was also—but I began to feel a sort of awakening. My first reaction was to question myself. Was I unconsciously sending out vibes? Was attending evening events without my husband a signal? Today I recognize that self-inquiry as a typical pattern of women, a self-doubt induced by a culture that presumes male dominance and privilege.

Around that same time, however, I also recalled a few other subtle signs of interest by contemporaries. A look, a comment, a touch that lingered too long. Writing this in the wake of the #MeToo movement, these memories—and my reaction to them—become more confusing than they seemed at the time. The unwanted advances in the darkness of a car clearly crossed a boundary, and I resisted, while the subtleties I detected from a few contemporaries stirred me in an entirely different way. Like me, all these men were married. The cultural undercurrents of the sexual revolution were evident in Boise, and divorces were not uncommon among our friends. My marriage seemed ho-hum. I craved the intellectual energy that can emerge from conversations about shared interests. I found that in my work life and with friends and began to sense that a merger of sexual and intellectual energy was a possibility, that a personal relationship could be forged based on mutual respect, intelligent conversation, and physical chemistry.

The *Statesman* was not a tightly run newsroom. The city editor counted on his reporters to suggest stories, giving us an unusual degree of freedom. I took advantage of that to cover some environmental stories of interest to me. An acquaintance who was the husband of a good friend had an intriguing story idea: Drive together to Henry's Fork, one of the nation's finest fly-fishing streams, for a story about efforts to have the area preserved as a state park. He would provide photographs and I would write the story. The city editor authorized the trip and off we went.

Henry's Fork, a branch of the upper Snake River, is more than three hundred miles from Boise. The trip would require an overnight stay. I saw it as a ride to a new part of the state for a good story and had no reason to suspect my traveling companion of ulterior motives. I didn't have any motives other than getting an interesting story and seeing a new part of the state. If Ken was suspicious, he didn't say so.

My memories of our work together in a stunning corner of Idaho near Yellowstone National Park have been lost to an evening of White Russians, a steak dinner, wine, and a seduction that had me reeling the next morning. This was the comingling of intellectual electricity and sexual energy I had imagined was possible. We continued to see each other in a cheap rented room in Boise for the next five or six weeks.

During that time, I compartmentalized my life and behavior. As the early thrill of the tryst began to wane, a voice crept into my head, asking, "What am I doing here?"

One night after cleaning up the kitchen and putting the boys to bed I went into our bedroom where Ken was sitting on the end of the bed. He reached around behind him and held up a small round flexible item.

I stiffened. "What's that?"

"You know what it is," he said quietly.

"It's my diaphragm. What are you doing with it? Where did you find it?"

I knew exactly where he had found it and I flushed with anger.

"Why was it in your purse? Why are you carrying it around with you?"

I didn't answer. If he'd gone looking for it, I assumed he knew—or suspected—everything.

"You've been seeing someone, haven't you?"

I nodded.

"Who is it?" He named our friend.

Again, I nodded.

"Do you love him?"

"I'm not sure. I might."

As soon as I said that and saw the pain in his eyes, I knew I did not love the man I had been seeing. I also knew I did not love Ken, but I cared that I had hurt him deeply, and it was the same kind of hurt that the man's wife, a good friend, would suffer. Even today I remember feeling awash in a cascade of consequences caused by my actions, consequences I felt immune to in the heat of an affair with the only man other than Ken I had ever been with. Over time, that brief affair has stuck in my mind as a sordid interlude for which I still bear a residue of shame and regret. My actions affected two marriages, several children, and a friendship. It's as if I had, for months, stayed in the alcoholic haze of the wine, White Russians, and sexual and intellectual stimulation; only upon being discovered did I sober up.

I sat down beside Ken and vowed not to see the other man again. "I'm sorry, I really am so very sorry," I told him. Ken turned away and didn't say another word all evening.

I felt awful but knew that what I had said was true. I would not see the man again, and I didn't.

Ken had good cause to ask for a divorce, but he did not, probably because of the children, although we did not discuss the possibility, and I didn't ask, instead maintaining equilibrium by moving ahead. We had already decided to buy a house in Boise's desirable North End closer to where the kids would go to school, and we continued that path. It was a bungalow that needed some fixing up, which we never seemed to get around to, but it was roomier and more livable than anyplace since Italy. Settling into a city neighborhood with sidewalks, alleys, leafy trees, and a convenience market and a park nearby satisfied a long-held goal of mine to experience the wholeness of in-city life. I grew up in a semirural suburban area and longed for a home with a real sense of place. Now I had just that. The boys went to an old brick elementary school a few blocks up the street. Afterschool care was available nearby, but Matt and Tim were unhappy about some of the rules.

"Mom," Tim said in a voice filled with disgust, "she won't let us take our Oreo cookies apart!"

"Really?" I asked, thinking that was a bit extreme. Matt asked me to talk to her. I was sympathetic, but declined to take up their case, suggesting perhaps they could make it themselves. They failed. I bought Oreos and we ate them any way we wanted, whole or—usually—separated.

Through my work, Ken's fishing, and our circle of friends, we had become avid environmentalists in Boise. In the sixties and seventies, Idaho was rife with political struggles to preserve enclaves of spectacular landscapes; often the threats were from powerful mining interests accustomed to getting their way, helped by cooperative politicians and lax state and federal laws. Despite our interest in the environment, our actual use of all the exquisite outdoors around us was modest. Hiking in the mountains was something we would get to someday, an aspirational notion.

While partying with friends early in 1974, we talked wistfully of getting into the Sawtooth Mountains, an epic mountain range in central Idaho that rivals the Tetons for spectacular, snow-capped, jagged peaks. After years of controversy, environmentalists were celebrating the passage in 1972 of legislation that created the Sawtooth National Recreation Area. "Wouldn't it be great to hike there and see it up close," someone said. Soon the talk turned serious, and three couples, including Ken and me, had committed to a summer backpacking excursion.

Despite my eagerness to join our friends, I had a private concern. By then, I knew that for me, the marriage was over, but I had not yet had the conversation I needed to have with Ken. Our years in Boise were a time of personal and professional growth for me. I began to reimagine a future like the one that disappeared the day I learned, as a college student, I was pregnant. I craved a more dynamic personal life.

Late one evening, a few weeks after we committed to the backpack trip, the boys went outside to play, and Ken and I lingered at the dining room table. It was time to break my silence; I couldn't maintain the veneer any longer. I moved the used dinner plates to the side and took a sip of water. I hadn't prepared a preamble; I got right to the point.

"I think you must know by now that I am not happy in our marriage."

Ken picked up his napkin and refolded it, keeping his head down. "Yeah, I guess I do know that, but I don't understand why."

"It's just not working for me anymore," I said. I took another drink of water. I told him how much I loved my job, the people I met through work, time spent with friends. "But at home I feel like a different person. When I walk through the door the energy dissipates." I stood up, looked out the window at the fading light, and, with my back to Ken, whispered, "No joy here."

"The kids? No joy?" he sounded hurt. It was a fair point, and I told him so. "I look forward to our weekend outings with them, but at home I feel a void, a lack of intensity. I need a fuller life than that." He asked if I was talking about divorce. Yes, I said. Ken folded and refolded his napkin, silent, head down. And I knew it was settled.

"Okay if I go and get the kids?" He nodded and I moved to the front door, quietly closing it behind me as I left to find Matt and Tim.

A few days later, after Ken found an apartment and was ready to move out, we talked to the kids. We told our friends of the separation; I assured them the backpack trip was still on, that there was no acrimony between us, and we were excited to go.

THERE ARE FORTY PEAKS OVER TEN THOUSAND FEET IN elevation in the Sawtooths. You don't see them often while hiking through the spruce and fir forests. As you climb higher toward the alpine tundra, the vista occasionally opens, and there they are—a line of spires reaching toward the sky, usually with a lake in a rocky bowl below. I was having a wonderful time, enjoying the exercise, the views, the camaraderie of friends, the discovery of wild onions to add flavor to the freeze-dried evening meal. Ken and I didn't spend a lot of time together, but I was comfortable with him there and sharing a tent. He was having some trouble with blisters, apparently because his hiking boots were not yet properly broken in. At stops he pulled out the moleskin, cut new patches, took off his shoes and socks and gently removed the old patches atop the blisters.

Late in the afternoon of the second day, our friend Wally, the logistical planner for the trip, invited me to sit with him on the boulder where he perched, gazing into the lake below. I joined him, and a companionable silence settled in around us. "Are you having a good time?" he asked, breaking the quiet.

"Oh, yes. I really love this." I told him the exertion, the air, the great views, being with friends was exactly the way I had imagined the hike.

"How do you think Ken's doing?"

"Well, he's having a blister problem, obviously. But I think he's fine." I didn't know where this was going. Wally was a successful businessman who scheduled meditation into his day, and I admired him for his quiet thoughtfulness. I readied myself for whatever it was he had to say.

"Mindy, I know you and Ken have split up. We all know that, but you are here with him, and I don't think you are being very kind to him."

I didn't know what to say. I studied the rock we were sitting on, looked across the lake to a craggy peak, thinking about Wally's observation. He was right. I *had been* impatient with Ken's fussing with his blisters, with how it slowed his pace. I was avoiding interacting with him or assisting him. Had I so distanced myself from him emotionally that I felt no empathy?

Finally, I responded. "Thanks, Wally. I get what you're saying. I'm being kind of a bitch, huh?"

"I didn't say that," he said softly, "but if that's what you're thinking, maybe you can do something about it."

I tried; I really did try. I stayed with Ken on the trail for much of the remainder of our hike, asked if I could help with his blister treatment, sat with him at most meals and tried to engage him in the glories of the Sawtooth wilderness. As usual, my enthusiasm was met by his quieter appreciation. If I said, "Wow!" he said, "Yeah, pretty nice."

Absent Matt and Tim, there was little to share, and, at best, only a subdued joy in the natural wonders all around us.

Soon afterwards I called a lawyer friend who agreed to handle our divorce. Like our marriage, it was amicable. Idaho had adopted no-fault divorce laws a few years earlier for circumstances such as ours—nonadversarial endings. I would remain in the house with Matt and Tim, Ken would see the children whenever he wanted. Besides the house and a car, we had no other assets. I had a steadier, if modest income, and was prepared to buy a car for myself while Ken's financial support would help with house payments. Nearly ten years after that trip to the Gresham courthouse in Oregon, the marriage was dissolved. We had two fine sons to show for it and, ultimately, lasting good will for each other. For me, it was freeing. I didn't celebrate but felt a mix of relief and anticipation for whatever the future would hold.

At the *Statesman,* the longtime political editor was planning to retire, and I had hopes of replacing him. I knew my way around the state legislature and political scene but was passed over. Angry and disappointed, I left the newspaper for a public-relations position at a land-use-planning agency, where I soon discovered I did not like being on the "other side." I missed the energy of the newsroom. When I learned that the political editor job was going to a staff member with no political reporting experience, I was even more miserable at my new job. I suspected that the fact the new editor was a man had something—probably everything—to do with it.

Then I got lucky. Maybe it was fate, which I don't believe in, or just being in the right place at the right time. I got a phone call from a producer at the Boise public-television station, KAID, asking if I would join the team creating a new nightly news report on the Idaho state legislature that would air live. I jumped at the opportunity. I knew nothing about television, but I did know about the legislature. I soon learned it was not that simple. The opening day of the legislative session I was live on the air, frozen behind the microphone, cameras rolling, my mind desperately scrambling for words to describe the scene. I felt like a color announcer for a football game who has forgotten everything he knew about the teams taking the field. I was so dreadful that even Ken called to commiserate and tell me he was sure that I'd soon get the hang of it.

Early in the spring of 1975, a man named Bill Berg showed up for work at KAID. I had met him a few weeks earlier when he came for the job interview, and now he was back to meet his new colleagues before taking over the next day as program manager. He was accompanied by his wife and small son, who was perched on his shoulders. I was looking forward to having him as my boss. He seemed like a guy who would be easy to get along with, and since he was trained in television, I assumed he would help me become more proficient as a television journalist.

I couldn't know it at the time, but Bill's arrival marked the beginning of a new life for both of us.

BILL

1975–1977

B ill started his job at KAID on a dewy-fresh spring morning brightened by daffodils across the Boise State University campus. Back then, the television station was on the first floor of a red brick building on campus, near the river. Now it's in another part of town, and I recently toured the modern facilities of this new station, no longer affiliated with Boise State. On the main floor were light-filled offices; below were several studios, up-to-date editing equipment, and a large archive of tape-recorded programs from earlier years, including some of mine from the mid-seventies. The workspace of my era was far different. The only natural light was at the front door that opened to the reception area and the station manager's office. Behind were several small windowless offices lining the hall that led to the studio and production spaces, editing rooms, and a workshop for building and storing sets used in the various programs produced by KAID staff.

Bill was the new program manager, the number-two position in station hierarchy. He would supervise the small staff of people involved in local productions, including me. His first morning on the job began with a tour by his boss, the station manager. As they passed my office, Bill stuck his head in the door for a friendly hello, and, while I sipped cold coffee, surprised at the tingle running up my spine, he recalled our meeting in the same office two months earlier after his job interview.

All these years later I can still hear a voice in my head saying that my life might get a lot more interesting with this guy around. Two brief meetings and already something was stirring in me. *You're crazy*, I told myself as he moved on down the hall. *Get back to work.* But as the morning progressed, I found excuses to head to the studio space where Bill was talking to directors and operators. Several cameras were scattered over the concrete floor in position for the next live program. Bill noticed me and invited me into a conversation about projects we were working on.

Why was I paying so much attention to the new guy strolling through the TV station? I asked myself. I was recently divorced, had a job I loved, had two kids, and was committed to staying single for a few years. For the first time in my life I was independent. I wanted to discover what it felt like to be on my own, raising the boys, making my own decisions.

As Bill talked to others, I saw a smile fill his face and send crinkles around his eyes. I noticed his quick wit and easy banter, even as he did more listening than talking. He took extra time to chat with secretaries, set builders, and janitors, and I liked that. He seemed kind as well as charismatic. I liked the way he moved with a slightly swaying stride, shoulders upright and held back. Some might have thought it cocky, but to me, his posture and pace signaled energy and optimism. I caught myself wanting to get better acquainted. Nothing wrong with getting to know my new boss, I told myself. Then another voice cautioned: Be careful; don't complicate your life just as you're beginning to enjoy your independence.

It was like standing in the middle of a seesaw hearing dueling voices at either end.

MY MOTHER WAS IN TOWN FOR A VISIT SHORTLY AFTER Bill came to KAID. One day we planned to go out for lunch but first dropped by the station so she could meet some of my coworkers, including my new boss. We walked down the hall to my office. I introduced her to the station manager and to Jeff, my co-anchor on the nightly legislative program she'd seen on TV the previous evening. We found Bill in the studio, where he made a point of walking over to meet Mom. He leaned in close to say hello and shake her hand while putting his other hand on her shoulder. I watched her smile and look up at him as he asked about her life in Oregon. When she told him about her seven daughters, he stepped back in surprise, grinned and asked her if they were all as pretty as me. Oh, the charm!

Later, Mom and I went to a nearby restaurant called the Ram and found a booth. Mom scooted around to the back and I settled beside her. A perennial dieter, she busied herself with the menu full of burgers and fries and fish and chips, shook her head, and sighed. We ordered salads and iced tea and talked about the people she'd just met.

"Bill seems very nice," she said, emphasizing *very*.

"Good judgment, Mom. He is nice."

"Is he married?"

"Yes," I said firmly. "And I'm not interested." I was not about to share with Mom my dueling voices.

"Well, he seemed interested in you." I pushed back from the table and stared at her. "Really? How would you know that?" I'd never thought of Mom as being particularly intuitive about romantic impulses. Fairly or not, I didn't think she understood much about my life at thirty-two. I had spent much of girlhood in search of my independent self, and had steered my own course, always trying to be a good daughter, if not a close one. Certainly not one who confided in her mother.

"Besides," I reminded her, "he's married." End of story for her.

THE DISTANCE BETWEEN US WAS BOTH EMOTIONAL AND geographic. As my younger sisters grew up, Mom seemed more relaxed about motherhood and more in touch with the three youngest girls and my older sister, Becky, who lived closer and saw her often. Like me, my eldest sister, Judy, had moved farther away. I was the first daughter to divorce, Judy was second. Others—ultimately six of seven—would follow. Over those years, our mother didn't judge us. Instead, she stayed devoted to daughters who matured into women so unlike herself. It was unconditional love that I failed to reciprocate. Much later, as heart disease weakened her body, and a less than fulfilling relationship with Dad eroded her spirits, I felt a deep sadness for her, but even then, could find no intimacy with my mother.

Mom and Judy had often argued. Once when I was about to walk into the downstairs playroom, I heard their raised voices. I couldn't tell what the argument was about, only that it was intensive. I halted, heard a slap, and Judy gasped, "What!" Then my mother's soft voice, "I'm sorry,

Judy." Mom was crying. I slipped away to my bedroom down the hall and quietly closed the door. I was shaking, stunned to my core. I vowed right then that I would never do anything to make Mom slap me.

Before I encountered that scene, I could not have imagined such a thing. Despite a house full of girls, there was little drama, at least before I left for college. I never saw Mom and Dad argue. Sometimes, out of sheer aggravation or impatience, Mom would raise her voice to stop an argument between two squabbling little sisters, and occasionally even give a swat to the bottom, but not to me, never me or Becky. We were people pleasers, not troublemakers. My tendency was to stay out of the way and not get involved. After overhearing Mom slap Judy, I took it as a lesson in how *not* to find my place in the family. Judy had made it clear she wanted to move away after high school, maybe become an airline hostess or a travel agent. Her life didn't work out that way, but at the time I admired her poise and ambition, if not her argumentative nature. That slap reinforced my determination to go quietly about my business. I would be a good girl.

Sitting in that booth with Mom, drinking iced tea, I was happy about having taken an important step—divorce— toward a future where I was in the driver's seat. We didn't talk about that or keep on with the conversation about the new guy at work, and I tried not to think about him. Instead we talked about Matt and Tim. Mom cared deeply about her grandchildren, and talking about how my boys were settling into life after divorce—and a pending summer visit with Grandma and Grandad—was easy territory for us as we finished our lunch.

WHILE I TRIED TO DISMISS BOTH MOM'S REMARK ABOUT Bill's interest in me and my own early heart flutters, I had a problem. Within weeks of his arrival, Bill began asking me out for lunch. Committed to a plan that did not include romantic entanglements, I put the lunch invitations into the category of a friendly, let's-get-acquainted offer. After all, he was married. But, yes, I told myself, I'd like to get to know him better. Often, I had other plans and declined, but within a few months Bill and I were having lunch at least once a week, usually with Jeff. The three of us shared an interest in politics and current events and enjoyed rousing lunchtime conversations. Sometimes it was just the two of us at lunch and I began to look forward to those occasions. As we became better acquainted and shared our life stories, I felt my resolve slipping. Once, Bill told me about listening to Pacific Coast League baseball games as a young teen. "Me too!" I said, remembering sitting with Dad listening to the Portland Beavers. I convinced myself that our shared interest in baseball had special meaning. The warning voice in my head fell silent, even shutting out the fact of his marriage.

Our favorite lunch place was the Ram, where Mom had said, "He's very nice; he's interested in you." Yes, I think that's right, I told myself, recalling a few times I felt bathed in his soft gaze. I wanted more of that, more of the laughter we shared. I looked forward to being with him, just the two of us. I told a few friends about him. My closest friend was worried because I was so recently divorced. She told me it sounded like I was being swept off my feet "by a charming playboy from Los Angeles." I laughed and told her she didn't know what she was talking about because she hadn't yet met him. "Besides," I said, "he's married." I promised to introduce her, but I didn't wait for her approval. Being with Bill felt right.

One day in early summer before any of this had been openly acknowledged between us, Bill invited me to take a ride after work. "How about Lucky Peak?" he asked. I sensed this was more than a casual drive, and I was eager to go. It would be our first time alone together outside our booth at the Ram. We headed to the reservoir created in 1955 by construction of a dam on the Boise River, and named after a nearby mountain peak. The Boise River drains a portion of the Sawtooths in Idaho's rugged central mountain region before making its way through the city of Boise and on to its rendezvous with the Snake River near the Idaho-Oregon border. I tried to disguise my jittery anticipation with calm conversation. We chatted about our work and colleagues as Bill drove along Warm Springs Avenue out of town, past the penitentiary; soon the road became Highway 21 and headed into the bare brown hills that loomed over the valley. About ten miles from town, where the reservoir appeared, Bill pulled into an overlook. "I've been looking forward to spending some time like this with you," he said as he turned to look directly at me.

I couldn't think of anything clever—or romantic—to say, although my pounding heart was signaling romance. I whispered the few words that came to mind: "This is a nice spot. I like getting out of town."

Bill put his arm around my shoulders, letting it rest there, not yet an embrace. "You must know I've become very fond of you."

"Yes, I guess I do know that," I said, struck by his use of the word *fond*—a nice old-fashioned word that did not come so easily to my lips. "I like you, too," I managed.

Bill pulled me gently to him and I responded. We embraced, kissed—tentatively at first, then with growing passion. I relaxed into the moment, pulled away, looked at him: "I liked that," I said. He touched my breast; I brushed his hand away. I needed time and distance to process what was happening, to compare these roiling feelings to my plan to stay single and unattached, to discover who I was on my own. "Use your head, Mindy," I said to myself, "before it's completely overtaken by your heart."

As Bill drove down the hill, I told him, "I think we should take this slowly."

"Sure, this road is a little curvy; I'll slow down." He put his foot on the brake and with exaggerated slowness, rounded the next curve. "Slow enough?" he asked, turning to me with a big smile.

"Smart ass. You know what I mean."

Even in my mellow state of euphoria after the moments we shared at the overlook, my "go slow" suggestion was genuine. However real my emerging feelings for Bill, I wasn't sure I was ready to get deeply involved with the first guy who came along. I had imagined a period of what I thought of as "having a life," enjoying being an eligible single woman, which I had missed in my twenties because of a quickie marriage and children. That image was rapidly fading, but even more important was the fact that Bill was still married, or I assumed he was. I did not want another affair with a married man. I didn't see myself as "that kind of woman." Despite the distance from my mother, I hadn't lost touch with her values. Although she had liked Bill, when she learned he was married, that was the end of the conversation for her. I, too, felt I had to put some brakes on.

"What about your wife?" I asked as we neared Boise. He told me the relationship had been over for a long time, and now he was ready to do something about it. He gave me the short version of his six-year marriage, and talked about his son, Justin, the sweet-faced toddler I'd seen perched on his shoulders when he visited KAID with his wife. I'd noticed then that Justin had Bill's curly hair and his mother's big, brown eyes. The story sounded familiar—a marriage of two people who were not well suited to each other in either interests, temperament, or energy. Bill told me he had been on the verge of asking for a divorce when he picked up his wife at the doctor's office and learned she was pregnant. His story had faint echoes of my own first marriage, based on an ill-timed pregnancy.

We continued our workday lunches and arranged a few daytime outings on weekends as our friendship evolved into a romance. Within a few months, and a few questions from me— "When are you going to split?"—Bill separated from his wife. He remained in the home they had rented on the bench beyond downtown Boise; he had agreed to keep Justin while his wife, who remained in Boise, searched for a job. Bill had no trouble finding good childcare, which amazed me, since arranging suitable care for Matt and Tim was a constant concern for me. Several of his neighbors were Mormon stay-at-home moms who were more than happy to help the nice-looking newly single dad next door.

I went to Bill's house occasionally and got to know Justin, who was then about sixteen months old. I also noticed Bill's approach to childcare: affectionate and matter of fact. Messy diaper? Stand the kid on the bathroom counter while water runs in the bath, remove offending diaper, and put the child in the tub. Bedtime? Read a few books, put him in the crib. Play time? Let his black lab, Carnaby, take over.

Lucky for Bill, Justin already showed signs that he had his dad's even temperament and was a remarkably easy child. He was just starting to talk, and he called me Mimi. We corrected him: "Say Mindy." He would grin and say "Mimi." We repeated it with the same result each time, and we all laughed, especially Justin, as if it was his little joke on us. My lifelong attachment to Justin began in those months.

I was not yet ready, however, to introduce Bill to Matt and Tim. They were then nine and six and still adjusting to the realities of divorce. I thought they needed more time than a toddler like Justin for that adjustment, and I wanted to be certain my relationship with Bill was more than just an exciting fling before I brought him into the mix. At this point Bill was newly separated, but divorce proceedings would not begin until his wife had found a job and resettled.

Bill didn't ask about meeting my kids. I didn't think anything about it at the time, but I realize now his apparent lack of interest reflected his attitude about children. Slowly I came to understand that for all the attributes we share, a genuine affection for children is not one of them. It didn't take long for me to realize that Bill's interest was in me, the woman he saw as smart and energetic, not me as a mother and the children that came with that.

As we spent more time together, the child issue was not front and center. Matt and Tim's father was in town, and they saw a lot of him. Bill and I didn't live together and were not yet projecting a shared life, and certainly not imagining what it would be like to be stepparents. When Bill's wife moved to Burley, a town two and a half hours away in southern Idaho, he took Justin there to live with her. I asked him how he felt about that, and he said he'd miss him, but also that his life would be simpler.

Bill's freedom meant more time together, and I decided he should meet Matt and Tim. One evening I told them I had become good friends with a guy at work who was going to stop by for a visit. "Is he like a boyfriend?" asked Matt, already suspicious.

"I guess you could call him that," I said. The boys played it cool when Bill showed up, politely answering his questions about school and things they liked to do. For all his ease and charm around grownups, to my kids he was just another adult. Matt soon asked if he and Tim could take off to see friends.

Having passed the introduction hurdle, I began to plan occasional outings with the four of us. One beautiful spring day we went for a drive into the desert for a short hike among the jackrabbits and spring blooms. Bill and I got in the front seat and Matt climbed in the back. Tim was slow to get dressed and was still on the front porch tying his shoes. Matt was anxious to get going.

"What takes him so long? He *always* does this."

"It's all right," Bill said. "We're not in a hurry."

Finally, Tim got in the car. "Slowpoke," said Matt, clearly intending it as an insult.

"You think you're so perfect," Tim said, raising a fist as if to punch Matt.

Worried this could escalate, I suggested each of them move to the far side of the of the seat. "No touching!" I said.

Bill gave me a surprised glance that seemed to say: *We haven't even started yet.*

All was calm as we drove out of town toward the Bruneau Desert. Bill suggested the boys start thinking about where they wanted to have lunch on the way home.

"McDonald's, McDonald's," shouted Tim.

"I'm tired of McDonald's. Let's find someplace new," Matt suggested.

"I like that idea," said Bill. "We'll look for a place later."

Tim began to pout. "No fair," he said,

"Just be quiet," said Matt.

"Don't tell me what to do," said Tim, stretching out to kick Matt's leg with his foot.

The squabbling continued, despite my call for a cease-fire.

Suddenly, Bill pulled over to the side of the road and stopped.

"Hey fellas," he said. "We're not going anywhere until the fighting ends." His voice was calm and steady.

I gave Bill a surprised look, then turned around to look at the boys. They stared at me, then at each other and remained still. We sat there in awkward silence for several long minutes. Finally, Bill, in his friendliest voice, asked, "Everybody ready to go?"

More silence. He started the car and we were on our way again. I glanced over to Bill and whispered, "Why haven't I thought of that?"

As an only child, Bill was puzzled by sibling rivalry. He is also an even-tempered problem solver who can fix just about anything. He *fixed* the car incident, but there would be more moments in the future that wouldn't be so easily managed.

AT WORK, I WAS IMPRESSED WITH BILL'S TELEVISION production skills and imagination about new projects. We were producing a variety of public-affairs programs, from coverage of the Western Governors Conference in Sun Valley to interviews with noted people of the region, including William Stafford, then the poet laureate of Oregon, and Jack Hemingway, celebrity fly fisherman in Idaho and son of famed novelist, Ernest. For me, it was a new kind of journalism, not based on news and headlines, but on what television does best—tell stories about interesting people, places, and events. Our work together became an integral part of our relationship, a professional partnership in which we learned from each other even as romance flourished.

We settled into a close and comfortable relationship, equal parts intimacy and friendship, and spent as much time together as we could manage.

A highlight of our last year in Boise was a weeklong trip down the Oregon Coast. By then, Bill had met my father and most of my sisters. Earlier, as we were getting acquainted, he had talked about his coolness toward his mother and explained why. She had grown up in a well-to-do Jewish family in Montgomery, Alabama, and brought her family's attitudes about race and class to Los Angeles. Bill rejected all that her upbringing was about, and described her as a "Southern Jewish princess" more interested in social status than academic achievement. As a result, he said, grinning, "I was raised to be charming, not sincere"—a mantra he has repeated over the years, a signature of his self-deprecating humor. I had seen him work his charm on Mom in that first meeting in the KAID studio, and his engaging personality had become a surefire path into the hearts of my father and sisters, if not my sons. It also helped that he was quick to learn and recite—whenever asked and sometimes just to show off—the names of all the sisters, in order: JudyBeckyMindyJennyRobinChrisandSusan.

Having been drawn to the ocean since I was a little

girl, the week Bill and I planned in Oregon was particularly meaningful for me. I saw it as a building block of our relationship—round-the-clock togetherness and shared decision making. I looked forward to what I would discover about our relationship along the way. I didn't think of it as a test at the time, but in retrospect, I suppose it was. Would my growing certainty about this relationship withstand all this time together? Would I encounter any regrets about giving up my newfound, but short-lived independence, for this man?

A friend had given us a small batch of marijuana for our trip. Knowing our inexperience, he had neatly rolled it into a few joints and sealed them in a baggie. Late in the afternoon while sitting around the campfire we decided it was time to find the baggie. We had borrowed my parents' tent trailer and put it to good use earlier that day, so we were feeling plenty mellow already. A few tokes, doing my best to inhale, left my throat feeling slightly raw, but the rest of me relaxed beyond mellow and into silly. We saw images in the fire and cracked up describing them—misshapen animals, our boss at work looking vicious, two people kissing. "That must be us!" One laughing spasm led to another as the afternoon devolved into senseless hilarity, an afternoon of sex, drugs, and rock and roll. Yes, rock and roll. We had a theme song, "Afternoon Delight," by Starland Vocal Band, a hit of 1976, which we played over and over, singing along, our voices soaring in bad harmony through the chorus—"skyrockets in flight, afternoon delight." I experienced—in that one day—what I had missed in the cultural revolution of the previous decade. Then, as a young mother in a new marriage on an army base in Italy, all of this was unimaginable.

To me, Woodstock was merely a vague reference to a gathering in 1969 of hippies smoking pot and listening to music. Summer of Love had something to do with young people taking over San Francisco in 1967. A few years ago, I saw a documentary about that gathering and mused about my life with a toddler in Italy during that time. What could have inspired those young people to hang out in Haight Ashbury? I had become an Elvis Presley fan in the late fifties but knew little of a group called the Grateful Dead. Crosby, Stills & Nash was familiar only later, when I became a fan of Neil Young and learned he had once been a part of that group. Laughing around the campfire, the closest Bill and I were to the pop culture of the era was our similar hair-styles—curly hair grown out in soft afros.

One photograph captures the essence of the trip for me. I am sitting at a picnic table in the glow of a camp lantern, finishing up the Dungeness crab that just a few hours earlier had been alive in the tank at the fish market. I look relaxed and happy. And why not? It was one of the finest days of my life. The sound of the ocean was ever present in the background. The smell of campfire smoke mingled with the damp earthiness of the forest floor. Cedar boughs hanging overhead dripped with accumulated mist left from the day's rainfall. Bill had cooked the crab to a perfect soft, sweet chewiness. We dipped it in melted butter that we licked from our fingers. We lingered there late into the evening listening to night whispers blend with the soft laps of a receding ocean tide.

DECISIONS

1976

B ack in Boise a few months later, I faced a crisis. For some time, Bill had been talking about frustrations at the television station. He liked the job itself and the work he was doing with me and Jeff and others. But Bill and his boss, the station manager, had very different styles, a personality clash that was making Bill miserable. The boss was there to stay, so Bill began looking for another job. I wasn't happy about this emerging scenario, but I knew Bill well enough by then to understand his need for a different job, a place he could grow and be more independent. By then we thought of ourselves as a couple and wanted to stay together. I encouraged him to look in the Northwest, suggesting that would make it easier to plan a future.

One warm autumn evening after work, Bill suggested we take a walk through the neighborhood, Boise's North End, near my house. It was a mix of older houses, including modest bungalows like mine and well-kept, two-story homes with wide porches and lush landscaping. After Bill's ex-wife moved with Justin, he had rented a small apartment in a run-down old house a few blocks from my home. As we headed for a street with fancier homes, Bill was unusually quiet. His silence told me he had an agenda.

Finally, he stopped. "You know that job I told you about?"

"The one at WXXI in Rochester?"

"Yeah, I told them I would take it."

"Wow, really? We haven't talked about it very much." My pulse quickened. I took a few steps back, put my hands on my hips and stared at him, shocked that he told the Rochester station before talking to me about the offer.

"Well, I did mention it, and you said you thought you could get a job with a newspaper there." He was right. I knew he was considering an opening, and I had told him Rochester was not as far-fetched a destination as it might seem. It was the headquarters of the Gannett newspaper company. I had some contacts in the corporate hierarchy through my earlier work at the Gannett-owned *Idaho Statesman*. In those days, not many women were yet working in newsrooms, and I thought I had a pretty good shot at landing a job there. But that was all abstract, rational thinking; I was not prepared for this surprise announcement that made it suddenly real. I felt left out of an important first phase of decision-making—talking it over, exploring the ramifications for *both* of us.

We began walking again as my words tumbled out. "I thought you were going to look more in the Northwest, ask at the Boise stations. Why does this have to happen so soon?" I was desperate, asking questions to which I already knew the answers, not wanting to confront this new reality: Go with Bill or stay with the boys? Continue a relationship that seemed so perfect or revert to life as a single working mom in Boise? Expand my career horizons or stick with the status quo? It was all a jumble in my mind, and I was unable to express what I was feeling—a sense of imminent loss, the slipping away of a relationship that was the source of the deepest contentment I had ever known.

"You know how I feel about my current situation," he said. "This is such a good opportunity for me. I didn't think I could turn it down."

I stopped again. Standing beside a white fence surrounding a stately home in this neighborhood I was so attached to, I fought back tears. "Why didn't we have this conversation first? I feel left out of a very big deal."

As Bill fell silent, tension built inside me; I could barely breathe. I looked at the house, the fence, the sidewalk, everywhere but Bill. "Where does this leave me? Us?"

A few weeks earlier we had talked about the prospect of maintaining a distant relationship if Bill got a good job offer far from Boise. He was certain it wouldn't work. He insisted that time and temptations would eventually erode what we had together. He knew his own need for companionship and was equally sure that other men would be as attracted to me as he was and that, in his absence, I would eventually succumb. I was the romantic to his realist and told him what we had was more enduring than that, and that I was committed to our relationship, even if it meant a separation for a year or two. I wasn't imagining at that time the distance would be so great; I was counting on him finding a job in the Northwest.

Having accepted a job in Rochester, three thousand miles away, he now pleaded with me to join him. I told him I needed to think about it. "You know how big a decision that is for me—it means leaving the boys."

He stared at the ground. "Yes, I know," he whispered.

We began a slow, silent walk back to my house. At the front door, instead of an embrace, I suggested he go to his place and I'd see him the next day. I opened the door. "Hi, Mom!" The boys were back from the park and bounded toward me; it was time to fix dinner.

————

WHEN I'D FIRST BEGUN TO CONTEMPLATE MOVING WITH Bill for new jobs, I never considered taking Matt and Tim with me. Any move would be about starting a new life with Bill and building my career. I could not imagine uprooting my children from their father, neighborhood, schools, and proximity to both our families for the sake of my new life. I was unwilling to admit an equally true factor, that I could not imagine beginning a live-in relationship with Bill as a working couple raising two children together. Although we never discussed it, I knew that Bill was not interested in being a stepfather, and I didn't want that, either. In those few months after Bill accepted the Rochester job, I tried to imagine what it would be like to be a part-time, far-away parent—regular phone calls, having Matt and Tim for long visits in summers, traveling to spend Christmas holidays together. Ken had remained an active father, seeing the boys frequently on weekends, and we maintained a cordial relationship. When I broached the idea with him of moving back into the North End home with the boys, he seemed more than willing to become a full-time single father. All this made it possible for me to imagine a new scenario.

Bill and I were in our early thirties—I was thirty-three and Bill thirty-one—and our careers were important to us. As I faced the prospect of a move—no longer an abstraction—I began to see professional advantages for me in working for a larger, well-managed newspaper. I was still the more consistent breadwinner for Matt and Tim, and that was a factor.

A friend once told me that I should operate more out of my heart than my head. I understood what she meant. In a crisis, big or small, my first tendency has always been to stay calm and figure out next steps. Whether the hurt is physical or emotional, outbursts are not in my DNA. There are no drama queens in my family of seven sisters. Now, facing Bill's departure, I calmly carried on, examining the options. Logic and reason were my refuge. There was no point in arguing with Bill. Neither of us likes to argue, even less to make a scene. It was one reason we were so comfortable together. His mind was made up; now I was making the plans necessary to implement my own decision.

Shortly after Bill moved to Rochester, I had sought and received an invitation to travel there for an interview and a tryout at the Gannett-owned *Times Union*. After spending a few days in Rochester with Bill and feeling good about the interview and story I had produced during the tryout, I had a calm confidence that I would be offered the job. I left Rochester with a date to start my new job at the beginning of the New Year.

Upon my return to Boise, I gathered Matt and Tim at the dining table and told them of my plans and that their father would be moving into the house with them after Christmas. They knew I had gone to Rochester where Bill was and that I had interviewed for a job. I tried to emphasize how little would change for them. It was hard to gauge their reaction. They knew I'd be around for a while, and busy boys focus on today, not the many tomorrows. A few days later we went with a photographer friend to have our picture taken. I told them I wanted to be able to see their happy faces when I woke up in the morning and before I went to bed. That photograph still rests on my bedside table.

Upstate New York was a world away from Boise, Idaho, and Cedar Mill, Oregon. I was ready to begin a new life there with Bill, assuming we would return within a few years to the Northwest, to good jobs nearer to Matt and Tim. I was sure the boys would be okay living with Ken— he was a good father, caring and capable. They would be attending the same schools, playing with the same friends. I didn't yet register the psychological impact on them of my leaving, but—ever the optimist—I was confident we could work through it.

I was writing in my journal during those last weeks of 1976, and recorded both the emotional turmoil and, despite that, my certainty about the rightness of my decision:

December 18: I'm feeling some of the emotional strain of leaving creeping up on me.

December 22: The mix of emotions is very real right now.... But always there is Bill, and not once have I had a second thought or moment of regret, even doubt, about what I am doing.

ON CHRISTMAS, KEN AND THE BOYS AND I ENJOYED A mellow holiday together at our North End bungalow. We'd never put much furniture in the living room, and I hadn't changed that after Ken moved out. It was play space for the kids; adults gathered around the dining room table just steps away. Christmas morning, we sat on the living room floor amidst piles of wrapping paper scattered all around. Matt and Tim were putting together the new Hot Wheels racing set. A case of Matchbox cars had been investigated, also the Lincoln Logs. The Slinky and yo-yo were somewhere under the paper. The boys inspected their new treasure chests first, announced that they were "pretty cool," and then moved them off to the side to open the toys and games that were more appealing.

"Let's walk to Camel's Back," I said. It was one of those cold, sunny days that I loved about Boise's winter. We'd had about an inch of snow, not enough for sledding, so the kids needed to be persuaded. "Come on," said their dad, "it'll be good for you." Ken and I knew it would be good for us, too, helping to move the day along toward the conversation I wanted to have now that my departure date was almost upon us. This seemed like the time to say some things left unsaid in the conversation weeks earlier about my decision. We hadn't talked about it much, just in matter-of-fact ways, with an occasional reference to "after I leave," or "when you are gone." Same house, different parent seemed to work for all of us over that period.

I had no outline for this new conversation. How do you explain to an eight-year-old your love for a man who is not his father? Your determination to pursue a career opportunity? You don't. All I knew was to try to make this day a happy one, and an honest one, by confronting the reality of a new future and the sadness we shared about the looming separation. I hadn't made a big deal about having a conversation with them on Christmas Day, and, with both parents in the house, they seemed to be savoring the family moments more than thinking about a fractured future.

We bundled up. "Race you, Mom," said Matt as soon as we left the house. And we were off, Tim and Ken in hot pursuit. We climbed up the steep slope of Camel's Back Park until we were out of breath, then headed home. Ken and I went into the kitchen to prepare one of the kids' favorite meals, spareribs and artichokes. We added a holiday touch with sweet potatoes and a jellied cranberry out of a can.

After the late afternoon meal, we moved back to the living-room floor. "Okay, guys," I said, "time to talk about what's about to happen." Before I knew I would be leaving, I had applied for a loan to upgrade the house, adding a third bedroom and second bathroom and remodeling the kitchen. The work would start shortly after my departure. Once I had decided to take a job and join Bill in Rochester, the pending house remodel fit neatly into the scenario I concocted for leaving the boys. Not only would they be with their father in the same home, but it would be a fixed-up home.

On Christmas Day the remodel was a big deal, not as big as me moving away, but easier to talk about. I asked the boys if they were ready for the building crews to invade their space.

"Yep," said Matt. "I think it will be cool to see how they do it." At eleven, Matt was already showing signs of the engineer he would become. Whatever emotions he had about my departure, he kept to himself; outwardly he seemed accepting and ready to carry on. He reminded me of myself, calm and resolute.

"I'm sorry I'll miss all that remodeling mess," I said.

"Then why don't you just stay," Tim mumbled. He was across the room, sprawled on the floor, alone.

"Oh, Tim, I'm feeling sad about this, too. Come over here and sit with me." We weren't a huggy family, but Tim used to like to cuddle, and he needed some of that now. So did I. Tim's gloom overwhelmed me, deepening my understanding of the magnitude of my decision. He moved slowly, slithering across the floor, and sat beside me. I held him tight, whispering in his ear, "Who do you think should get the new bedroom?"

"I don't know. It probably won't be me," he said, immune to efforts to cheer him up. A feeling of helplessness overtook me. Still holding Tim, I leaned back against the wall, silent.

Ken intervened. "We'll work that out later," he said.

Ken's cooperation made all this easier than it might have been. Our deal was that I would continue to make house payments, which included the remodel, in lieu of child support.

I stood up and suggested we go sit around the dining room table. Once we'd settled there, I turned to the bigger issue of the day, telling them that next Christmas they would be with me at Grandma and Grandad's in Oregon. I described the apartment in Rochester where the boys would visit in the summer. "It has a pool," I said. "We can get bikes, ride to a nearby park, and explore the neighborhood." Kids live in the here and now, and none of this seemed to mean much to them.

The boys' eyes turned to the living room, now cleared of wrapping paper, where toys beckoned. Matt spoke next. "Can we play with our Christmas stuff now?"

ROCHESTER

1977–1979

F lying out of Boise early on December 29, 1976, I was numb, drained of all emotion and thoughts. I went through the motions—get ticket, check luggage, find my gate. On the plane I took my seat by the window. As the plane took off, I watched as the snow-covered valley disappeared, soon replaced by folds of mountains and deep river canyons. The plane ascended through clouds into a vast featureless space, nothing but white below and blue sky above—a world as empty as I felt. I took out my journal: *I just can't write what I feel right now.*

After changing planes in Chicago for the flight to Rochester, I found some words: *More sadness than excitement. I can't think about what I am doing—have, in fact, done— without tears tempting to burst out of somewhere. I knew this would be hard, but the knowing is not the living, experiencing, feeling.*

I didn't want to arrive in a puddle of tears. In the weeks leading up to my arrival, Bill had not sounded like himself in our phone calls—no quips, none of his usual humor. Instead, I sensed in him an anxiety about my ability to settle in and be content while separated from the boys. As the plane landed, I fretted about spoiling a reunion he had been anticipating for many weeks, but there was nothing I could do; I was drained of all emotions, nothing left for Bill. I was trapped in a time warp, immersed in the past and unable to imagine the future. The present didn't exist for me that day.

BILL WAS PATIENT AND UNDERSTANDING, SENSITIVE TO my inability to verbalize my feelings of sadness and loss. Two days later, on New Year's Eve, we went to a nice restaurant for dinner—candlelight, wine, music. I tried to rally, but that evening lives in my memory as little more than a valiant attempt at normalcy, a genuine effort to regain the intensity of the emotional connection we had established in Boise. A week later, I returned to my journal.

> *January 6, 1977: I feel not quite whole. I miss Matt and Tim a great deal and must be sure to occupy my time so that I don't have too many empty moments to feel the pain of the separation. The worst is knowing that they, too, now realize what has happened. Tim's tears on the phone were just about more than I could bear.*

As I had suggested, Sunday-night phone calls became a part of our weekly routine. So did Tim's tears, at least in the early months. Each time was a reminder that these kids, especially Tim, were hurting. And so was I.

During a Sunday phone call a few months after my departure Matt said, "Guess what, Mom?" I thought it was a game and played along: "Okay, what?"

"I fell on Camel's Back and broke my wrist."

"Oh, Matt! Are you okay?"

"Yeah and guess what else—I broke my other wrist."

The distance from Boise might as well have been a million miles. I was helpless. But Matt was not finished. "Guess what else? I broke my collarbone, too."

Despite the injuries, he sounded fine. I had never been the kind of mother who fussed over cuts and bruises or called the doctor when the kids were sick. When he was six Matt broke his elbow while playing at day care. He spent three weeks in the hospital with his arm raised in traction. Mom came to spend time with him while I worked, but, best of all, the summer Olympics were on television. Matt was a good little patient and had no permanent damage to his arm. These new injuries seemed mild in comparison. Being so far away, there was little I could do other than trust Ken and believe Matt when he told me he was patched up and feeling fine. He seemed happy to finally have something interesting to say in the weekly phone call. Like me, he didn't like chatting on the phone. Tim was more purposeful, writing out a list of the things he wanted to tell me to make the most of our long-distance time together.

Nevertheless, Matt's tumble on the slope was a vivid reminder of how far away I was from both boys and how little impact I could have on their daily life, safety, and care. I talked to Ken, who told me Matt really was fine despite the injuries, which would heal within two months. As I'd suspected, Ken told me that Matt had wanted to tell me on our regularly scheduled Sunday phone call rather than immediately in a call from his dad. At eleven, Matt was old enough to call some of his own shots, and I trusted Ken to know what I needed to know—and when. I was sensitive to my status as what I came to call the "away" parent and didn't feel it was either necessary or appropriate to set new ground rules for our communication. Sunday night was our weekly touchstone, and short of a genuine emergency that didn't need to change.

Even so, the phone call made an impression. Through one child's tears and the other's injuries I came to realize I was wrong about a few things. This separation was a lot harder than I had anticipated. Despite all my careful planning, my children were not "just fine," nor was I. Not really. Not yet. Having created what seemed like such a simple, tidy arrangement—substituting one parent for another and expecting everything to be okay—I had fooled myself into trusting my rational, well-planned approach, all the while ignoring the possibility of emotional stress or trauma. For all my efforts to minimize the disruption of my boys' lives, there was no way to minimize how much my leaving would disrupt their hearts. Or mine.

LEAVING THE BOYS MAY HAVE BEEN FORECAST IN 1969 during the first months after we'd returned to America from Italy. Shortly after beginning my newspaper job, I knew—as surely as I had ever known anything—that full-time, stay-at-home motherhood wasn't right for me. A more satisfying marriage would not have filled the need I had to be out in the world—even the small world I had entered in Lewiston, Idaho. There were no role models for the path I found myself on, a consequence of circumstance and choices. The cultural revolution of the late sixties did not penetrate my consciousness during those three years in Italy, and it certainly wasn't apparent in an out-of-the way place like Lewiston. Nor had the nascent women's movement reached me. Mary Tyler Moore as a spunky TV journalist was still several years away. My life and dreams had been interrupted by pregnancy and marriage that coincided with college graduation. In Lewiston, the need to find a job and make some money put my life—if not my dreams—back on track. Dreams remained forgotten, restored only later, after Bill.

By 1976, facing a move with Bill to faraway Rochester, I confronted what had been a theme of my post-Italy life: balancing motherhood and career. The equation was complicated by loving a man I did not want to lose and knowing he felt the same about me. At ages eleven and eight, the boys' worlds were expanding, and they were more capable, spending the bulk of their days in school. The heavy lifting of early childhood was over, and they were less dependent on me. At least, that's what I told myself. They were close to their father, and his willingness to be the full-time parent sealed it for me. The boys would be well cared for in a familiar environment. And yet.

Yes, it was tidy, missing only the emotional component of a mother's intense love for her children and their all-important attachment to her. Using the logic of a good team leader, I had created a plan for how this would all work out. Now a mysterious something, a less-used emotional center embedded within, was sending danger signals. In those early weeks in Rochester, I cried more than I ever had and slept less. I didn't think about undoing everything and going back to Boise. I'd made my plan and was moving forward. But a new awareness of the connectedness of me, Matt, and Tim was forming, an awareness that would shape future decisions.

As winter and my grief descended, romance was my balm. Being with Bill was everything I had imagined—daily conversations about our jobs and colleagues, making meals together, planning weekend sightseeing. Rochester is famous for harsh winter weather, and Bill and I soon encountered it. We often stayed indoors playing Scrabble, one game after another, tournament style, sprawled out on our apartment floor. I won more games than Bill. "It's luck," he said. "You get better letters."

"Oh sure," I said. "Don't you suppose maybe I'm just better at figuring out what to *do* with my letters?" When Bill won, he'd announce his good luck and say, "It must be time for sex." Once, we prepared tacos to eat during our tournament on the floor. Bill must have won, because after we put the board away, Bill began to make familiar moves. We stripped, and—suddenly—a stinging sensation. "Yikes," I cried. "What's that? Hot sauce?" We still chuckle at that memory.

Our jobs went well, but Rochester held no charms. Locals were not used to people moving in from anyplace west of Buffalo. Friendships that came so easily in Boise were hard-won, if they were won at all, in Rochester. Accustomed to the energy of an up-and-coming town in the West, we found ourselves in a provincial northern city, a company town that revolved around Kodak. We were on new terrain, emotionally and physically, as we mapped out this new place in our relationship.

A few weeks after I arrived, a record-setting blizzard paralyzed the region. It disrupted the life of the city but did wonders for my emotional recovery—I got outside and turned the weather challenge into an adventure. We put on cross-country skis and took off to explore our neighborhood. Getting lost in a huge nearby park—and finding our way home after dark—added an extra thrill to the day.

Spring arrived, and we began to explore our new terrain. We took off in Bill's little Ford Pinto and explored upstate New York, especially the Finger Lakes region. We became runners and learned to appreciate Genesee beer. When you are virtually alone in the world, it is a good thing if your lover is also your best friend. Would this, could this relationship last? I began to hope for the long haul.

It didn't take long, however, for me to conclude that I couldn't stay in Rochester more than a few years. Phone calls were inadequate. Matt and Tim and Justin came to Rochester for summer visits, and I spent Christmas in Oregon with my boys, while Bill visited Justin. Every departure led to intolerable teary goodbyes at an airport. As my relationship with Bill flourished, I realized that it wasn't full-time motherhood I needed, but proximity. I had to be close enough to be able to see Matt and Tim more often and for us to feel more a part of each other's lives. I needed them back in arm's reach.

I gained confidence in the staying power of the relationship Bill and I had forged, even though we were not yet married, and faced the likelihood of withstanding more career moves together. Bill didn't share my optimism about this—not because he doubted *us,* but because he was rational about all things, including love. I even harbored the thought that the next move could be mine. I was confident I could find a job in the Northwest and that Bill would also find a career path back home. My need for that was so great I must have entered a phase of magical thinking, as I had no firm evidence to support my certainty about the future.

In the meantime, my career took a quick turn in Rochester with the election of Jimmy Carter. Early in 1977, Carter presented a list of expensive federal water projects he thought should be canceled. The biggest target was the Central Arizona Project—CAP—the largest, most expensive water-transfer project ever proposed. A new, 335-mile aqueduct would take water from the Colorado River to rescue farmers in central and southern Arizona who had, for years, been depleting their underground water sources.

This was a big and important story. "We should tell it," said Bill. He had a point: We *could* tell it. I was familiar with western water issues and well acquainted with former Idaho Governor Cecil Andrus who, as President Carter's Secretary of the Interior, was the lead cabinet member on implementation of the president's hit list of water projects. Bill was eager to dive into a significant television documentary project. And, more important, we had an angle: Make this a national story about government waste of taxpayer money to irrigate western deserts, *supposedly* for agriculture, but often for new golf courses and subdivisions with extravagant pools and fountains. I was eager to work together with Bill on a project of this magnitude. I relished the idea of spending part of the summer on the road with him, as both a life and work partner.

There was a problem. I already had a job. How could I take on a project that would put me on the road for weeks at a time? I tried to not get too invested in the idea, because the project depended on getting funding from the Corporation for Public Broadcasting. Bill submitted the proposal.

I was surprised and a little flummoxed when we got the money. What now? Bill thought there was some chance I could get a job with WXXI, his employer, which was sponsoring the project. There was no guarantee, but I took a chance, quit my newspaper job, and moved to a temporary desk at the station, diving into research for the documentary we would call *Even the Desert Will Bloom*.

Our documentary won a prize accompanied by a $10,000 cash award. We used the money for a down payment on an older home in central Rochester; it was a financial investment, not a sign of settling into the city.

Working on the documentary during that first summer in Rochester simplified time with the boys when they came to visit. I enjoyed a flexible schedule, and we spent a lot of time hanging out at the pool in the apartment complex. Thanks to the lifeguard, I could leave the kids alone for a spell to get some work done inside.

Other than gatherings at the pool, those few weeks with Matt and Tim and Justin are mostly a blur. It was the first time all of us were together, almost like a family, but it didn't feel that way. It felt temporary, because it was. When we weren't focused on the documentary project, Bill was with Justin and I was with Matt and Tim. None of us seemed ready to figure out during that brief time in our suddenly cramped two-bedroom apartment what this stepparent, stepchild thing was all about. Days passed quickly, and the visit ended with hugs and tears in the airport.

At the end of the documentary project, WXXI hired me as producer and anchor of a five-night-a-week newscast. My television skills improved enough that as I began to plot finding a job in the Northwest, I thought I might have a shot at commercial television, which had more news jobs than public TV. As I pondered the future, I realized that even if my on-air tapes were adequate—and I wasn't certain they were—television didn't feel like a career home for me. Even on public television, with smaller, more serious audiences, female anchors get frequent comments about appearance— hair, clothes, smiles—and it grated. I thought of myself as a serious journalist, and increasingly, as a potential editor or team leader in a newsroom. After television jobs in Boise and Rochester, I had become more confident, not just as a journalist but as a woman with skills and experience prepared to succeed in the professional world. Bill's support and encouragement along the way was integral to how I felt about myself as I made my choice: Return to print.

I was happy to be working with Bill again in jobs that suited us. After the documentary was shipped off for distribution to PBS stations, we returned to our favorite weekend pastime—exploring the countryside of upstate New York.

"How about some beer?" Bill said as we started out on an early trip.

"Sounds a little naughty, but sure," I said. Inside the roadside market, Bill got a six-pack of Genesee and I picked up a bag of Oreos. "Don't you think these would be good with beer?"

Bill gave me a mischievous grin and put the cookies on the counter beside the beer.

It was the start of a bad habit as we traveled the roads of upstate New York, west to Niagara Falls, and east to the Adirondacks and Lake Placid, where construction was under way for the 1980 Olympics.

Over the years Bill and I have done some of our best thinking and planning while driving hundreds of miles in a car together. For me, taking a long drive with Bill is a reminder of the singular importance of my Rochester years, a time of separation and coming together. I was away from the boys and with Bill, experiencing that relationship in splendid isolation and creating the emotional scaffolding for the future. Alone together we got to know each other better, love each other more, and grow respect for each other's independent nature. And always there was laughter, which I have come to believe is the secret sauce of a good relationship. It was preparation for a life together going forward—hard work, geographic separations as we pursued independent careers, ups and downs as parents and step-parents, and more than a little luck.

The second year in Rochester I flew to Oregon for my family's Christmas gathering at the Oregon coast. Bill was with Justin in Idaho. The boys and I were excited to be going to the beach, always a special place for us, but especially so this year because we were having a family reunion with all six of my sisters and their families. Afterwards, the airport departure was the hardest ever. I struggled to hold back tears, walking briskly toward my departure gate where the boys and my mom would see me off, expending energy, moving to avoid talking, unable to verbalize the pain I was feeling. Hugs were all I had to give them. A family reunion at the beach is as good as it gets in my family, and Matt and Tim seemed to enjoy it as much as I did. Emotionally wrenched as the plane took off, I told myself, "Never again. No more airport goodbyes." And I meant it. Back in Rochester I told Bill, "I can't do this anymore." He knew it was coming. I had given two years to Rochester and a life with Bill. I wanted our life together to continue, but not in Rochester.

I wrote a letter to a friend in Idaho who was working for my former employer, publisher of the *Lewiston Morning Tribune*, and asked about job prospects. I was surprised to see a letter from him in the mail just a few days later. He made no reference to the letter I had sent him but started right off asking if I would be interested in returning to the *Lewiston Morning Tribune* as managing editor. Our letters had crossed in the mail.

Sitting on the sofa in our Rochester house I read in disbelief. My heart beat faster, my hands shook; I leaned back, rested my head on the high-backed sofa, and closed my eyes. Could I be this lucky? I am not a religious person, but if I were, this is exactly what I would have prayed for.

Ken and the boys had recently moved from Boise to Sandpoint, a small town in the Idaho Panhandle that had attracted hippies and back-to-the-land folks throughout the seventies. Ken was not of that ilk, but he had friends who were, and he believed in the environmental concepts that fueled the counterculture lifestyle. It was a good place for him to set up a new optometry practice.

The most important point for me was that Sandpoint was 160 miles from Lewiston, close enough for frequent weekend visits. Nearly as important was the job itself. A decade earlier I had left the *Tribune* as a young reporter headed to Boise with two little boys and a husband. Now I would return as managing editor. It was too good to be true, but it *was* true. Things were falling into place for me. I hoped—and *believed*—that Bill would find a way to follow. In the meantime, I would go ahead.

TWO YEARS AFTER MY TEARY FLIGHT FROM BOISE TO JOIN Bill in Rochester, I kissed him goodbye, climbed into my white Pinto station wagon, and headed west. The ache of leaving Bill behind was leavened by my eagerness for a solo road trip. As I drove, I recalled that earlier journey and how changed I was from that time. I thought about the road trips Bill and I had enjoyed in upstate New York, drives fueled by beer and Oreos, me separating the cookies and scraping the cream filling with my teeth, while Bill devoured his in two crunchy bites. I recalled the Scrabble games on the floor, the intense time together on *Even the Desert Will Bloom*, how our relationship had flourished in the last two years. Mostly, though, I thought about my good luck and my new job.

I planned to meet my mother in Denver and visit my sister, Judy, in Colorado, and then drive with Mom to Portland for a short visit and finally to Lewiston. My solo route took me through the fields of Kansas and plains of eastern Colorado. I began to see the faint outlines of the Rocky Mountains, lines that grew sharper and higher with each mile. The more the mountains loomed, the more my spirits rose; I was back West again.

———

SIX MONTHS LATER, ON A SWELTERING AFTERNOON, I left the *Tribune* office and headed for the parking lot, where I broke into a big smile as I spotted a can of Genesee beer on the hood of my car. Bill had arrived, finished for good in Rochester. He had gotten a job at the University of Idaho, teaching broadcast journalism and working for the small public television station. I hurried to my rented apartment up the hill and walked into Bill's open arms. We were together again. And my boys were just a few hours away

LEWISTON

1979–1981

L ewiston was not the town I had left ten years earlier. New dams on the Snake River had brought slack water and a new port to the region, along with barges that carried loads of grain hundreds of miles downriver to the Pacific. At the confluence of the Snake and Clearwater rivers, where they hug the historic part of town, the city nestled below the water level, separated from its heritage by a huge dike. The Snake had been tamed and so, in some ways, had my love affair. Bill and I settled into the life of a professional, career-driven couple. I had been welcomed back at the *Tribune* as both a leader and colleague. From our apartment, Bill commuted thirty miles up the steep grade, away from the river through the sensuous rolling hills of the Palouse, to the University of Idaho, where he taught, and to KUID-TV, where he supervised local production.

On many weekends, I saw Matt and Tim. Ken met me at Plummer, halfway between Lewiston and Sandpoint. I greeted the boys, now fourteen and eleven, with hugs, and they hauled their bags from one car to the other while Ken and I chatted amiably. The boys loved Sandpoint, where they could swim and hang out at City Beach in the summer and ski at Schweitzer in the winter. Ken and I avoided any talk of changing our parenting arrangement. He had built his life around the boys, and with Bill and me now living much closer, I was content to continue the status quo. No one, including me, wanted another disruption.

I LOOK BACK ON THAT TIME AS A CONSTANT BALANCING act, life on a three-legged stool: work, Bill, the boys. The kids were near, but also far. The part-time reality of their presence didn't lend itself to developing household routines and family-like cohesion. To Matt and Tim Bill was more a benign presence than a stepfather fully invested in their lives. That seemed fine at the time; I welcomed Bill's focus on me and our relationship. But I wonder now if I missed an opportunity to create a sense of family. Matt was a teenager and Tim an adolescent, so it wouldn't have been easy, but I don't remember trying. Tim was occasionally difficult, stubborn and resistant to parental authority. A pattern developed: Bill would ask Tim to do something around the house, he would refuse, and I would intervene, trying to be the peacemaker, to maintain calm. Now I see these moments as stress fractures in a family that hadn't really become a family. Often separated by time and place, I hadn't developed the everyday habits that ought to have come with raising two maturing boys.

In seemingly insignificant moments over the years, I have been reminded of what it means to have been the away parent. I once watched Matt, a grown man with a wife and son and a good job, wielding a dust mop as he cleaned the hardwood floor of a new house Bill and I had just moved into. Struck by his efficiency with the mop, I observed him turning it strategically to hold the dust already collected while heading in a new direction to pick up more. I asked him where he'd learned that skill. "I used to clean Dad's office," he said. I stood still, silent, staring at the dust mop moving across the floor, realizing how little I knew about the quotidian details of the lives of the boys I had left behind.

A similar moment with Tim, then a father of two sons. I asked him what books he was reading to his kids now that they were past the age of *Goodnight Moon*. He mentioned *Watership Down* and *The Hobbit*. "Books I liked as a kid," he said. I had no idea he'd read those books.

I experience such moments as nostalgia for missing pieces in my life's puzzle, a lack of memories about the daily-ness of motherhood. What were their favorite television shows? Who were their favorite teachers? You can't ski and swim all the time—what else did they like to do? Ride bikes around town? Hang out with friends? Who were their friends and what were they like? Most mothers know such things.

Kids of divorce compartmentalize. I could have asked more questions about their life with Ken during their visits with me, but they were reluctant to talk about it, and equally reluctant, I suppose, to discuss time with me when they were at home with their dad. The same was true when Justin spent time with us. I was quick to pick up the cues and restrained my natural inquisitiveness around the boys, sensing their protective shield around the other parent. Also, avoiding emotional conversations was an easy choice for me.

I CAN'T SAY HOW, BUT MATT AND TIM KNEW I WAS THE one who ended the marriage. Maybe Ken told them, or possibly they figured it out through my actions and attitude. As they spent time with me and Bill, they witnessed our playful togetherness and easy contentment. They surely noticed the absence of tension, in contrast to Ken, whose stubbornness could shut down discussion. Whatever resentments they had about Bill—and I know they had some, particularly Tim—they were harder to sustain after extended time together. Even so, it was years before they fully accepted Bill.

Today I realize that, like the children, I, too, compart-mentalized, separating work and home, a pattern that persisted later, when Ken and I agreed that Tim, then an argumentative thirteen, should live with me and Bill in Seattle. I had to be at work at six in the morning, and it was months before I learned that Tim's neighborhood friends roused and got him to school most days. Tim was hard to waken, and some days they gave up. Only later did I learn from the school about the days he was tardy or missed class altogether. Looking back on the Lewiston period, I see how I could have been more in touch with the daytime dynam-ics among the boys, who were mostly on their own while I was at work a few miles away. I could have checked in at lunch, called home during the day, encouraged them to call me. Such connections are easier for today's parents, but not impossible, even then, for an attentive mother.

Years later, Tim confessed that he had taken out on Justin, who was six years younger, the injustices he had felt as Matt's little brother. At the time, however, none of that was reported to me or Bill. Justin was sweet and patient and not inclined to tattle. But once, after a summer visit in Lewiston, Bill got a letter from Justin's mother with vague references to some problems Justin had with Tim teasing him. By then the boys were gone and summer misdeeds forgotten, or, in Tim's case, reserved for confession years later.

Soon after Bill arrived in Lewiston, we started looking at houses, I was eager to round out our work and part-time parenting with a house and yard. We settled on a new house in a rapidly developing subdivision. It was on a cul-de-sac above the Snake River far from the smelly plume of the Potlatch mill on the other side of town. We couldn't afford a house with a view, but every trip to and from our new home took us along a road with a view of the river and hills to the west, which satisfied my need for wide-open vistas.

As a youngster I was bored by my parents' frequent trips to the nursery to buy plants for constant upgrades of the landscaping around the family home. Now, on weekends alone with Bill, there was nothing I'd rather do than head to the nursery to select plants for our new yard, a conscious act of our settling down together. We did every bit of the landscaping ourselves, from design to planting. Bill once told me that in the early stages of our romance he made a list of the attributes he wanted in a woman. High on the list was stamina. We had done enough hiking and running together to assure him of my energy level, but full weekends of side-by-side digging, hauling, lifting, and planting left no doubt that I had stamina and perseverance to match his.

Bill and I had worked well together on many projects, and in Lewiston, the house and yard became the blueprint for our life together, creating patterns of a shared domestic life. Planning and planting—ideas as well as grass and garden—was the core of what our partnership was all about. We were growing together, living fully in the present and preparing for the future.

At work, I soon learned that my most effective role was as a facilitator of a competent staff, and decision maker when necessary. I kept up the newsroom tradition of the daily critique, a public posting of what I judged to be the best work in the day's newspaper, and, when necessary, what fell short. When it was time to do the newsroom budget—a new task for me—I surprised myself with how easy it was to examine the numbers and come up with three scenarios—best case, worst case, and hold the line. In a newsroom accustomed to the bombast of the previous editor, I was a calm presence. Some reporters probably missed the drama, but I sensed that some of the quieter folks, especially a few less experienced women, welcomed the change.

Bill and I were making friends and, for what now seems like a brief interlude, we thought we might settle in Lewiston. The town was famous for its pink flowering dogwood trees, my favorite. We planted one in our new front yard, and I looked forward to enjoying it in years to come as its delicate, uplifted branches, cloaked in pink, would announce the arrival of spring. After years of just getting by, unsure of my future, I had dreams again.

We decided to get married. My mother adored Bill and couldn't understand why after more than four years together we were not legal. "When you get married," she told me, "I'll give you that small maple chest you like." The chest was one of the few items Mom and Dad brought with them when they moved the family from Ashland, Ohio, to Oregon in 1948. Mom was right; I had long coveted that wooden chest. Maybe it was that chest. Maybe it was the pleasure of our newfound domesticity, or maybe it was our active small-town social life among professionals who didn't know what to make of an unmarried couple like us. Probably it was all of that.

On January 5, 1980, at Mom and Dad's house at the end of a cul-de-sac in Beaverton, we put a tablecloth over the television in the small living room, set a vase of flowers on top and called it an altar. Standing before it, along with a family friend who was pastor of a local Congregational church, we repeated vows we had written ourselves. Our three boys were there along with Bill's mother, most of my sisters, and their families.

Only later did I reflect on how different this cheerful family gathering was from the furtive elopement fifteen years earlier. At age twenty-two, I'd lied to Mom to borrow her blue Lark and sneak off to get married. I'd never dreamed of a big wedding with white dress, flowers, and attendants, even though I'd been in a few. For me at age thirty-eight, as a mother of two and a self-assured newspaper editor, these moments in Mom and Dad's house on a chilly day in a new decade were perfect.

It was a warm family occasion. We shared our vows of love and respect for each other and Bill's goodnight kisses for all the available sisters ended the day in laughter. The day also brought the first taste of alcohol for Matt and Tim, who sneaked at least one glass of champagne each. So jolly was the mood that no one—not even teetotaler Mom—noticed or cared.

Married, with a house, jobs we liked, and lots of kid visits, we felt settled.

THE ELECTION OF RONALD REAGAN LATE IN 1980 changed all that, altering the political landscape in Idaho as well as Washington, DC. Questions about funding for public television prompted talk of cutbacks and consolidation. The floor under public television in Idaho began slipping away.

Soon the life I had made in Lewiston, my balancing trick on the three-legged stool, began to tumble and fall. It was a dizzying time. With funding eroding, Bill gave up on public television and found a job as reporter/producer/anchor for a newsmagazine that aired Sunday nights before *60 Minutes*, a good fit for Bill's talent and experience. There was one drawback: It was in Yakima, Washington, some two hundred miles away.

Yakima is not a job destination to brag about. A mid-sized town in an agricultural valley of south-central Washington State, it felt to me like a place progress forgot, a town that earlier in the century had the choice of a state fairground or a college. City fathers chose the fairground. It was not a career step up from Lewiston. Bill saw the job as a transition into commercial broadcast television, a possible jumping-off spot to Portland or Seattle. I was heartsick about the prospect of leaving Lewiston and being farther from the kids, but Bill and I were committed to sharing our lives together, and I understood that his need for career success was every bit as important as my own. I was not excited about working in Yakima, but I promised him I would try. After Bill accepted the job, I arranged an interview with the local newspaper, the *Yakima Herald*. It was positive, but nothing certain. About this same time, I was scheduled to attend a regional conference of newspaper editors in Seattle.

Today the unsettled period ushered in by Bill's new job runs through my mind like a fast-paced movie, a series of scenes, a surprise twist, and a stew of emotions—elation, anxiety, and despair.

I see the nondescript, drab duplex apartment Bill rented in Yakima.

I see myself engaged in lively conversation with half a dozen editors, all men, crowded into a van during the Seattle newspaper conference.

I am with Bill in Yakima; I tell him about meeting a van full of *Seattle Times* editors; he worries that I will leapfrog over him—and Yakima—and wind up in Seattle.

Back home in Lewiston the phone rings. A *Times* editor invites me to Seattle for a job interview.

I call Bill. We talk about the possibility of my getting an offer from the *Seattle Times*. Bill is anxious, dreading what he sees as a long separation and my entry into a stimulating new environment with all the temptations he assumes that would bring. I try to reassure him; I tell him I am committed to our marriage.

I am in the office of the *Times*'s executive editor, being interviewed by several editors, all men.

Later, another phone call at home in Lewiston. A *Times* editor offers me the job of associate city editor with the expectation that I will become city editor within a year or so. I accept.

I am elated. But soon my heart sinks, knowing that Bill will not share my happiness.

Today as this film loops in my mind, I tense up all over again at the memory of how Bill felt about my skipping over Yakima to a good job in Seattle. There was no softening the impact. At the time I was overwhelmed by the same sense of good luck and good timing that struck me in Rochester when the Lewiston job offer came. I was lucky to be a female with newsroom leadership experience just as the *Seattle Times* was looking to bring women onto the management team. I was lucky to have met *Times* editors at a conference when I was already contemplating a move from Lewiston. Luck and timing.

Bill assumed he could get a job in Seattle within two years and suggested I put the *Times* off in hopes they would hire me down the road, after he had a job there, too. I could not imagine risking this opportunity. Seattle was little more than a two-hour drive from Yakima, and weekend visits would be simple to arrange. Our conversations covered old ground: Bill's concern that I would be swept off my feet by some new Mr. Wonderful; my repeated assurances that I was crazy about him and in this relationship for the long haul, and that I had as much confidence in his career as in my own. Just as in Rochester I *knew* he would get a job in Idaho, I now *knew* he would soon be in Seattle.

Of course, I couldn't *know* any such thing. I am not prone to flights of fancy or making predictions. But for someone who lives more out of her head than her heart, this sense of knowing Bill's future came from deep within. Maybe it's best called *intuition*. I knew his talent and his tenacity. I knew that faced with the loneliness of separation he would make it happen.

STEADY, STEADY, I TOLD MYSELF AS I DROVE THE SIX miles of steep grade out of Lewiston. I'd said my goodbyes, put the for-sale sign in the yard, and found an apartment in Seattle. But as I made the twists and turns up the hill, I was overcome with a sense of unfinished business, a combination of anxiety about the unknown in Seattle and a sense of loss about leaving the comfort and security of Lewiston and easy-to-arrange weekends with Matt and Tim. At the top of the hill, two thousand feet above the Lewiston-Clarkston valley below, I stopped at the overlook, one of the most spectacular views in a state full of fabulous vistas. I got out of the car and stood for a long time, breathing deeply, finding familiar spots in the valley—the *Tribune* building, the college on the hill, the road along the river to our neighborhood. I thought of Matt and, especially, Tim. He was having problems at school and arguments with Ken at home. Ken and I had broached the idea of Tim coming to live with me in Seattle after I was settled. I said, "It's my turn," and a frustrated Ken was ready to hear that. Matt was doing well in high school and would stay in Sandpoint through graduation. The future was hazy with complications compared to the clear outlines of my past two years in the valley below. Everything was up in the air again.

SEATTLE

1981–1990

———————

On a summer day in 1984, the copy boy scurried into my small office, tossed the afternoon edition onto my desk, and left as quickly as he'd arrived. I glanced at the top headline, grabbed the newspaper, jumped up and strode out to the huge newsroom, past the rows of assistant city editors to the circle of copy editors beyond. Most were huddled over their computers, but the copy desk chief, final arbiter of front-page headlines, was standing, looking at the fresh-off-the-press page one.

"What's this?" I said, thrusting the six-column banner headline under his nose: *Mondale Picks Queens Housewife.* He raised his head and gave me a puzzled look, "What?" The copy editors had raised their heads and were now watching as I glared at their chief.

"'Queens Housewife'?" I said.

———————

When I started at the *Seattle Times* late in 1981, I was the first female news executive outside the features section. Others were hired in following months and years, but I was the one who protested the headline on that July

Mindy Cameron

day in 1984. Geraldine Ferraro, a three-term congress-woman from New York, made political history when Democratic presidential candidate Walter Mondale chose her as his running mate.

I was reminded of the time back in Boise when my editor explained why a colleague was paid more than I was for similar work. The response— "He has a family to support"—relegated me to little more than a housewife working for pin money. That reality of the seventies was immortalized by the popular *Mary Tyler Moore Show* when her character asked the same question of her boss, played by Lou Grant, who answered with an attitude that conveyed what a stupid question that was: "Because he's a man." The headline moment in the *Times* newsroom was a full decade later, and attitudes were little changed.

I headed back to my office and, sitting down at my desk, was pleased to see that the commotion I'd started in the center of the newsroom had drawn other key editors—all men—out of their offices. The final edition headline read *Mondale Picks Geraldine Ferraro*.

Women have changed newsrooms in many ways—from headlines to story selection to management style—but gains didn't come easily. I didn't know it at the time, but just as I was beginning my career in 1970, a small group of college-educated young women with dreams of being journalists sued *Newsweek* for sex discrimination. They had the same credentials as the young men who were brought into the magazine to write news stories, but the women were hired for menial tasks in the mail room or as fact checkers. By 1973, *Newsweek* had agreed to hire women for the writing staff. The slow evolution of newsrooms across the country was underway and finally made it to Seattle, where I was a beneficiary.

Before the Ferraro moment, however, I had gotten off to a rough start with my boss, Alex, and it was partly my fault. Before I left Lewiston in 1981, a *Tribune* reporter interviewed me about my new job. In the story I was quoted saying the *Lewiston Morning Tribune* was the "best newspaper I'll ever work for." The story was picked up by the Associated Press, and when Alex saw it, he approached me at the city desk, where I was talking to an assistant editor. He gestured for me to come over and held out the AP story. "What about this?" he said, scowling. I quickly read the story. "Oops," I said, taking it lightly, "I meant to say best 'small' newspaper." He didn't return my smile.

Alex was a force in the newsroom, and he looked the part—a bear of a man, not too tall, but as thick and sturdy as one of the Douglas fir trees that populate the forests surrounding Seattle. He had a beard and dark eyes that signaled more scowls than smiles—as I'd already learned. He inhabited the managing editor's office down the hallway from my much smaller city editor's office and across from the glassed-in meeting room, where editors gathered several times a day in what was called a "news huddle." That's when top editors from the newspaper's various sections decided which stories would run on the front page and which ones would be held for more reporting. Alex was a looming presence at those meetings, listening more than talking, and asking few questions as decisions were made. Occasionally he roamed through the newsroom, talking to his longtime colleagues and pals among the reporters and assistant city editors, ignoring others. He rarely came into my office to discuss stories or ask questions, certainly not to offer friendly advice.

I've always been a quick learner. Not a brilliant student, but above average and a good test-taker. I didn't have to push myself to get high grades. Early job successes had reinforced a sense of myself as an achiever, a journalist who didn't need a lot of guidance. Now, working in a more complex organization, sometimes I felt inadequate. I got to know city desk reporters and assistant editors and sensed a budding respect from most, but not Alex. His silence kept me off guard.

One episode came to be known as the "five-fuck memo." It may have been just four, but in newsroom lore it eventually grew to six or seven. I don't even remember the subject, but it had to do with a story I had approved that Alex didn't think belonged in the *Seattle Times*. When I arrived for my usual six o'clock morning shift, the story had been published, and Alex had already fired a note to me via the internal message system. I signed on to my computer, and there it was—something along the lines of, "Why the fuck did we do this fucking story; what the fuck were you thinking?" I was shocked and offended—not by the language—but by the angry tone delivered so impersonally. I should have barged into his office and asked for an apology. Instead, I cowered at my desk and showed the offensive note to a few colleagues, the worst possible thing in his eyes—looking weak.

I HAD BEEN AT THE PAPER ABOUT SIX MONTHS WHEN Bill got a job at Seattle's KING-TV and could finally leave Yakima. Until then we managed to be together most weekends. At his bleakest moments he predicted our story would not have a happy ending. I had refused to accept that and, once again, his dogged job search prevailed. The hazy future

I had envisioned as I left Lewiston finally came into focus in July 1982, when he moved to town. Bill's presence brought a much-needed light touch of humor back into my days and gave me a supportive ear when I needed to vent about Alex.

Tim, then thirteen, and Bill's son, Justin, who was nine, would soon arrive for the summer. As Ken and I had agreed before my move to Seattle, Tim would remain with me and start school in the fall. Ken had told me of his concern about some of the kids Tim hung out with, his slumping grades, and the arguments that arose over Ken's attempts to impose rules. Matt and Ken were getting along fine, and Matt wanted to stay in Sandpoint, play soccer, and finish high school. Bill and I had found a home for lease in Shoreline, north of Seattle, near a park on the edge of Lake Washington. Today that summer of 1982 stands out as a period of unusual equilibrium, the point when the bubble in a carpenter's level is precisely between the two lines. Finally, at thirty-nine, I was on solid ground, ready to be a wife and career mom with a child at home.

While Bill was still in Yakima getting ready to make his move, we had discussed parenting strategies, preparing ourselves for life in Seattle after Tim's arrival that summer. Bill thought of being a parent of a teenager as akin to living with an unreliable car, a kid who needs a tune-up—structure and rules. But I knew that Tim, a shy, moody, and often unhappy teen, needed more. I wasn't sure what that *more* was, but my gut told me it was more complicated than behavior contracts and clear consequences, the kind of advice you read in a book. But I agreed to start there.

The following spring, when the lease on the Shoreline house was about to end and Tim was finishing ninth grade, Tim and I spent weekends house hunting. One day we found a perfect-for-us house in Lake Forest Park, an established community nestled among mature evergreens near where we were living. It was a maze of hilly, curvy roads with homes ranging from elegant to ordinary and a few pockets of new construction. At the end of a cul-de-sac was a brand-new, three-bedroom home with a spacious, light-filled sunken living room. As we walked out the door, Tim and I looked at each other with big smiles and knew instantly our search was over. When Bill came to see it, he shared our enthusiasm.

It felt good to be settled. Soon, though, it became evident that Tim was not adapting. One evening, after not saying a word at the dinner table, he stretched out on the couch in front of the television in the small den adjacent to the dining room. Bill was outside in his garden. I asked Tim to join me back at the table; he shuffled over and slumped into the chair opposite me, facing into the kitchen.

"You seem unhappy," I said. "Can we talk about that?"

"Nah, I don't know what to say. It's all so different here."

"But you're making friends, aren't you? Do you miss your Sandpoint friends?"

"I guess so, a little."

"Do you miss Matt? Your Dad?

"Yeah, sorta, but I know why I'm here."

"Why do you think you're here?" I asked, hoping he'd say something positive. That it would be better for him, that I wanted him here to help him get a fresh start in school.

His voice lowered, almost a mumble as his chin dropped onto his chest. "Because Dad and I were fighting too much. Matt and Dad don't ever fight."

Uh-oh, I thought. Where do I go with that?

From the time they were little boys, it was plain to see how different Matt and Tim were. As soon as he could talk, Tim announced, "I'm the boss of me," and carried that attitude into his adolescence, resistant to anyone telling him what to do. Hard as I tried not to, I would find myself arguing with him. Matt was more easygoing and even-tempered. I am often reminded of the time my father told me, when comparing his seven daughters: "You were easy; you raised yourself." Looking back on the boys' teen years, Matt seemed to be raising himself.

"Do you want to be more like Matt?" I asked Tim. His head snapped up and he looked directly at me. "No," he said. I want to *be* Matt." My heart broke. To hear a boy, my son, wish himself out of his own body. What depth of unhappiness had caused that? And what could I do about it? I'd like to say I reached out to touch him, hug him, anything to make a wordless emotional connection. Instead, I saw the pain in his face, shook my head, and looked beyond him into the distance, out the front windows to the green shrubbery and the cul-de-sac in waning light. I don't remember how the moment at the table ended. I probably sat there as Tim got up and went to his room.

I'd hoped Tim's coming to live with me would give us time to grow closer. Now, it seemed, we were far apart.

Another time, an angry, profane Tim lashed out at me over some long-forgotten argument. Bill, working at the dining room table, reacted with an anger I'd never seen. "That's it," he said, standing up and rushing down the step into the living room. Tim was standing near the sofa, glaring across the room to where I was seated. Bill put one hand on each shoulder, pushing him out of the room and up the step toward his bedroom. Tim, his face blank, seemed stunned into silence. As he continued shoving, Bill told Tim he never wanted to hear him being disrespectful to his mother: "Never again!" Tim spent the remainder of the evening in his room.

I was no longer the away parent, but I hadn't figured out how to be the at-home parent, either, the mother Tim needed. It is clear to me now that I had addressed the distance in mileage by having Tim in my home, but still maintained an emotional distance as I concentrated on issues at work and Bill, the easiest part of my life. Unpracticed in the daily routines of parenting a young teenager—paying attention, taking an interest, chatting, participating, simply caring—I was failing at motherhood.

AT WORK, IT BECAME CLEAR THAT THE SITUATION WITH Alex was a predicament, and it gnawed at me. I saw no career path at the newspaper that would remove me from under his leadership. He was born and bred to be a *Seattle Times* editor, following the path of his father, a long-time, beloved newsroom leader. A few years younger than I, Alex wasn't going anywhere. After a few years, that realization prompted me to look for another job. A friend who had worked at the *Washington Post* arranged an interview for me. Once there, I learned the only position available was in one of the suburban bureaus. I was a forty-something experienced editor with no interest in a suburban DC job. Afterwards I realized it was a courtesy interview, and I flew home feeling like a fool for taking both my time and the interviewer's.

Worse yet was an interview for a San Francisco newspaper, also the result of a tip from a colleague. Bill and I flew down together, anticipating dinner out at one of the city's great restaurants after my interview and an additional day to enjoy San Francisco. I found the stately old building downtown, and the receptionist ushered me into a huge, dark office with walls of bookshelves that extended from the floor to what must have been fourteen-foot ceilings. The editor, whose last name was Hearst, was seated in a desk so big he looked like a small man, although he was of average size. Behind him heavy drapes over a tall window were closed against the day's sunshine. A few lamps cast the only light in the room. Despite having agreed to the interview, the editor wasn't sure he had a job opening. "Maybe I'll just reorganize," he said, and rambled on, naming staff members I didn't know. "I think he could be a good leader," he said of one editor. He didn't look at my resume or ask anything about my work experience. The meeting left me, once again, feeling stupid for being there.

That night at dinner I described the odd meeting to Bill. "That was way too weird," I said. "I'll stick it out in Seattle." Bill was supportive of my quixotic job search and refrained from offering advice, but his response—"good decision"—signaled his relief at the outcome. Later that night, I stood in the hotel shower, hot water mixing with my own tears as I flushed away unrealistic notions of one more career move to escape from Alex.

Today, when I think of that woman bawling in the shower, I'm embarrassed by her foolishness. Instead of settling in, finding allies, confronting Alex, and figuring out how to do the work I knew I could do at the *Times*, I had let one person get under my skin and tried to run away.

Back in Seattle I knew I had an ally in the newsroom's top editor, Mike, who had advocated hiring me. He and

Alex were reporters together earlier at the *Times* and rose through the management ranks to the number one and two positions. Despite their closeness, the two men could not have been more different: one a hard-nosed news guy native to Seattle, the other a visionary journalist from outside who would go on to earn an MBA and bring those skills into newspaper management. Mike's newsroom nickname was the Zen Master. It was often suggested that Mike was so nice he needed an asshole in the newsroom, and that was Alex's role.

Several months after my failed job search, I talked to Mike about my frustrations with Alex. Mike's view was if I couldn't succeed at the *Seattle Times,* that was Alex's failure, not mine. He soon told Alex as much and asked him to see an outside counselor to find out more about himself and his work style. He also told him to work things out with me.

Despite my dilemma with Alex, I had some success in the newsroom. Early on I began posting on the bulletin board a daily critique of the work of the city desk, much as I had done at the *Tribune.* A tradition at the *Tribune* was a startling new idea at the *Times.* I wrote a breezy note, which might cite the day's best lead paragraphs or remind reporters to do the math for readers, when necessary. Once, I chided the use of *elderly* to describe a sixty-year-old accident victim.

When Washington's Senator Henry (Scoop) Jackson died suddenly in the fall of 1983, my political instincts kicked in, and I took a lead role in assigning and editing stories to convey the legacy of his thirty years in the Senate. I regularly worked with reporters and assistant city editors to polish major stories. Also, suspecting some old-timers wondered if the new editor could write, I did a cover story for the newspaper's Sunday magazine.

Gradually, friendships developed, and on many Friday nights Bill and I would stay in town for drinks with a few *Times* reporters who especially liked to razz Bill as the TV guy. Now secure in his own profession and in our relationship, he was once again the often funny, engaging charmer I had fallen for in Boise.

ONE FRIDAY AFTER DRINKS, WE DROVE HOME TO TAKE Tim, then fifteen, to a high school dance, as promised. We left the car in the driveway and walked together into a dark, still house. "Tim," I called out.

Nothing.

"Look," Bill said, pointing to the door of the liquor cabinet in the living room, which was slightly ajar. I rushed down the hall to his bedroom, stopping at the open bathroom door, frozen by the sight of Tim passed out on the cold tile floor in a puddle of vomit. The stink overpowered a lingering minty odor of mouthwash and the man scent of antiperspirant and hair gel. Bill, who had followed me, had the phone to his ear calling 911. I felt the icy chill of guilt snaking through my veins. We were in a bar with friends while my son, home alone, was raiding our liquor cabinet. Horrible-mother thoughts entered my brain, clashing with bewilderment about what could have been going through Tim's head while he waited for us.

The aid car arrived within minutes. Tim, still unconscious, was lifted onto a gurney and carried out to the ambulance. Bill and I followed it to the hospital and watched as the medics wheeled Tim into a room just off the emergency entrance and hooked him up to fluids. A nurse assured us Tim was okay, and said it was best if we went home and awaited their call in the morning when he was awake.

I didn't get much sleep that night. The picture of Tim, seemingly lifeless on the floor, replayed in my head like a scene from a horror movie. A simple question reverberated: "What now?"

The call came shortly after sunrise. In the hospital room, Tim was dressed, but still in bed. He was sober and embarrassed. I leaned over, hugged him and told him how frightened I was to find him like that. Leaning in from the edge of the bed, I looked him in the eye: "Why?"

"I don't know how to dance," he said. "I thought some booze would relax me." I shook my head and mumbled, "Oh, Tim," keeping to myself concerns that my son's shyness was hindering his development. When Bill suggested dance lessons might have been a better plan, Tim gave him a wan smile.

The episode shook me. Bill and I had been planning a trip to Cancun, arranging for Tim to stay with a friend's family. "What are we thinking?" I asked Bill. The last thing Tim needed was for us to take off for a fancy vacation and leave him at home with friends. That question still rings in my head today as I write this. *What was I thinking?* I was still compartmentalizing, fitting Tim into the motherhood box of my life, not yet fully engaged as a mom, not closing the emotional distance. Full engagement became my goal: No more nights staying after work for a drink, more meals together at home, more attention to what was going on in Tim's life, checking in with school officials about his grades and attendance record. I was also confronting a reality. I loved Tim. I knew his sweetness and sensitivity and hints of the wry humor that would evolve as he became an adult. But often I didn't *like* him. Can a mother feel that way? Can she say it, even to herself?

The feeling was fraught with the reality that Tim had so many of his father's traits. I needed to separate my conflicted feelings about his father from feelings about my son. I knew Tim, a teenager, wasn't going to change anytime soon. I was the adult, and I had to change. I had to act out of love, give him more time and attention, try harder. Tim was interested in cars and food; I needed to set aside the newspaper or book I was reading and take time to listen—really listen—to him, learn what mattered to him and why. Years later, while preparing to be a facilitator for a training course called *Seven Habits of Highly Effective People*, I was struck by the simple idea that love is a verb. We talk about *falling in love* and *being in love*. But once fallen into that state, you don't stay there without persistent acts of love. That's especially true for a mother who falls in love with her child in the first instants of his life. Parenthood means daily acts of love—being there, paying attention, being emotionally engaged—things I had never learned properly to do after I became the away parent.

WITH MIKE'S ENCOURAGEMENT, ALEX SCHEDULED A meeting with me. His office was flooded with natural light from the wall of windows overlooking the busy street two stories below. Alex was seated at his desk at the end of the room, shirtsleeves rolled up, revealing his thick wrists and beefy hands. He immediately got to his feet, smiling. Gesturing toward the windows behind him, he asked, "Is that too bright? I can lower the blinds."

"Nope, never enough sunshine around here," I said, as I sat down in an armchair near his desk. Alex walked around his desk, stopping first to close the office door and sat in a chair facing me. We hadn't developed a habit of small talk or personal conversation but had discovered we shared a yen for weekend getaways from the city. "How was your weekend? Did you get to Idaho?" He was leaning back in his chair, the relaxed, genial guy I had observed in the newsroom touching base with friends. We chatted briefly about our weekends and then he mentioned his visit to the counselor. "I'm glad I went," he said. "I learned some things about myself. What would you like to know?"

"Oh, everything," I said, smiling, now at ease. "Tell me why you don't speak up in the news huddles. Your silence is off-putting. And do you know that you often seem to be scowling?"

"I'm thinking," he said. "I think to talk."

I told him he didn't talk enough and left many of us up in the air about what he was thinking. And, I added: "I talk to think." I explained that was my way of testing ideas openly, aiming for collaboration and shared decisions.

As we acknowledged our differences and the misunderstandings that could arise from them, I was struck by the changes in Alex's demeanor and how comfortable I felt in the moment. Was it the counseling? Mike's pushing him toward a new approach? My growing confidence? Whatever the influences, the meeting ended in a new and comfortable cordiality that continued for years.

COUNSELING WAS ALSO AN ISSUE AT HOME DURING OUR early Seattle years. At first it was just for Tim, for whom it didn't seem to make much difference. Eventually we tried something else—counseling as a threesome, a family unit.

I was edgy, not knowing what to expect, as we entered the counselor's office in a small brick building a few miles from our home. The counselor, a soft-spoken, middle-aged man with thinning brown hair, greeted us, introduced himself, and asked our names, and then ushered us into what looked like a living room with an adjacent office space. He suggested we all sit on the sofa, as he went to turn on a soft overhead light and a nearby table lamp. He pulled an armchair in front of us and sat down. "Tell me about your family," he said.

Sitting between Tim and Bill, I began to explain the complicated story of how we came to be here, emphasizing my concern that Tim often seemed unhappy. Bill added a few details, and mentioned he was troubled that Tim was sometimes disrespectful to me.

"And, how about you," said the counselor, turning to Tim.

Tim looked at the floor and shook his head. "I don't know what to say."

The counselor asked me how I saw my role. "I'm his mother. I'm trying to find ways for Tim to be happier here."

I had no experience with therapists, but I soon realized how skilled this one was at getting to the truth without following a straight line of questioning. He discovered that Tim and Bill rarely talked to each other and that I was the go-between, just trying to keep the peace at home. Suddenly, facing the counselor, I saw what he saw: We were not functioning as a family. I thought back to our summers with the kids and how we acted more like camp leaders than parents trying to knit a family together. We thought of our three boys as his-and-hers, never "ours." The message for me was clear and logical: Get out of the way; let Tim and Bill work out their differences. To Bill and Tim, he said, "Talk to each other." Looking at one and then the other, he said, "You live together and have to learn to understand each other. That can't happen unless you talk."

Those words were not magic bullets. Bill and Tim did not become chatty, but I sensed a gradual easing of tensions as we all did our best to put into practice what we'd heard on the counselor's sofa.

Tim's interest in food became a big part of his life, and I participated fully while Bill supported this new interest in food preparation. Home economics was Tim's favorite class in high school; he even took a second food-related course as an alternative to PE. Together we agreed that he could cook two meals a week as part of his duties around the house.

"Hey, Mom," he said one day. "Could I invite my home ec teacher to our house for dinner?"

"That's a great idea," I said. "What will you make?"

He was still for several minutes, thinking; then he smiled and said, "Crab crepes."

The dinner, which also featured a butter lettuce salad and a now forgotten dessert, was delicious. The teacher was impressed, and so was Bill, but no one more than I.

As our lives stabilized in Lake Forest Park, it was Matt, not Tim, who caused a brief period of concern. I saw him less frequently during those years, while he was busy with high school. We went to Sandpoint for summer visits, holidays, and his high school graduation, but he was a peripheral part of our busy Seattle lives. That distance was magnified for me during a recent Christmas visit when I saw a picture of Matt as a young teenager playing soccer. I hadn't seen the photograph before and was taken aback, realizing I had never attended a soccer game to see my firstborn son compete. How many times, as a grandmother, had I driven hundreds of miles, from my home in Sandpoint to the Seattle or Portland area, to see a grandson's baseball, basketball, or soccer game, or a swim meet?

Matt went on to college, but like many boys with no clear career goal, he couldn't figure out why he was in school. He craved a life with more adventure. Ken and I had continued to stay in touch about the boys, and we were aware of Matt's restlessness. Neither of us put up a fuss when he told us, at age twenty, he was going to Mexico to teach windsurfing. In fact, he was going to Mexico to windsurf; the teaching was merely a way to support the lifestyle. It was 1985. Weeks accumulated into a month or two, and neither Ken nor I had heard from Matt. Thoughts of Mexican jails filled with young American adventurers snuck into my head. Ken had the name of the area Matt had mentioned as a possible destination, but no additional contact information. I took that clue and a description of Matt—tall, skinny, dark curly hair, big brown eyes—to the newsroom and asked Tomas, a Spanish-speaking reporter, if he could help track down my son. I had a lot of respect for Tomas's reporting skills, but that respect turned to awe when, after a few days of sleuthing, he got a message to Matt that he should call his mom and dad. The Mexico adventure didn't last long, and Matt soon returned to the Northwest and to windsurfing, working, and eventually a college degree. But the pattern was set. Independent and self-reliant, Matt makes his own decisions, calls every few months, and visits several times a year.

BY ITS VERY NATURE, WORKING AT A DAILY NEWSPAPER is stressful—competition, deadlines, egos—but after our meeting, Alex was less of a factor in my workplace stress. We worked as colleagues and occasional collaborators. It became evident he trusted me to lead the city desk, as he focused on changes in other parts of the news department. Even so, I yearned for a new challenge, a role with more independence. In 1989, when I learned the editorial page editor would be retiring, I saw myself in that job. Like the editorial pages of most newspapers at that time, the *Seattle Times* editorial page had always been led by men with strong ties to the newspaper and connections to the city's power centers. The 1980s was a decade of change at the newspaper, and I had a hunch that change might now extend to the editorial page. I went into Alex's office to tell him I was going to apply for the position. He looked up from his desk and smiled: "Good for you. You'll be great at it."

At the *Times*, the editorial page editor reports to the publisher, not to news executives. Frank Blethen, a fourth-generation member of the paper's founding family, was four years into his role as publisher. I knew he was interested in shaking things up, but would he appoint a very different kind of person to run the opinion pages, someone—a woman—without an established profile in the community? I told him of my interest, and he was intrigued. There was no formal application, no outside search. Within a few days Blethen announced my promotion to editorial page editor. I called Bill with the good news. "We're going out to dinner, babe," he said. We toasted my new job and my departure from the Alex orbit. He was no longer my nemesis but, even so, it felt good to have earned my own newspaper domain.

About the time we located Matt in Mexico, Tim

was graduating from high school. It was 1986, and he thought it would be easier to get a job in Sandpoint, a more comfortable and familiar place than Seattle, which was big and booming in the late eighties. Ken had remarried and had a small house behind his home in Sandpoint that Tim could use. We emptied his bedroom and carried his belongings to his Ford Ranger. "My cat!" he said and hurried inside to find her.

I sensed Tim's excitement about returning to Idaho and silenced my concerns about his readiness for the future, and whether being so close to his dad was in the best interest of either of them. We stood in the driveway, stalling the inevitable departure with chatter about the six-hour drive to Sandpoint, the weather, his plans for job hunting. "Okay, get out of here," I finally said, giving him a tight hug. I watched with a tinge of melancholy and worry as he drove to the end of the cul-de-sac, smiled and waved, turned left, and headed for the freeway that would take him across the state.

I didn't realize it at the time, but I now know it was the beginning of Tim's entry to an independent adulthood. Our relationship was far from perfect; he could—and still does—provoke me into an argument, but those instances are now few and far between. As he matured, I liked the warm, witty, and sensitive person he was becoming. To this day, however, recalling memories of life as Tim's mother is hard for me, and it is the hardest part of writing this story. There are countless moments of joy, but they all rest on a thin layer of guilt, like an interior residue of the soul. For all the satisfactions in my life, a sense of many jobs well done, I struggle to dispel the notion that I may have failed Tim.

THAT NOTION—AND THE STRUGGLE—AROSE IN THE writing of this as I recalled a session with an industrial psychologist early in my tenure with the *Seattle Times*. Company policy required all management employees to go through a day of testing and assessment; management believed the results would help us better understand our work styles and motivations. Some staff members thought the practice was a little creepy, something like group think, but I looked forward to it. Not accustomed to deep self-reflection, I thought the assessment might be an easy way to learn something new about myself.

I remember being surprised at the end of the test day when a total stranger—the psychologist—examined the long list of my responses to multiple choice questions and described a person that sounded very much like me. He told me I had an aptitude for literary and analytical endeavors and a high interest in the outdoors. Among my main drives he cited self-actualization, leadership, competition, and recognition. He said I understood human behavior and had a sensitivity that led to tact. He suggested that I was well suited for the job I held, but also, much to my delight, he said I would have been a good forester.

I don't remember asking about it at the time, but over the years I have mused about the term *self-actualization*. As I began to write about my life, the term took on some urgency. What does it really mean? And what does it say about me?

In the world of human behavior, self-actualization is described as the motive to realize one's full potential, to reach self-fulfillment. Abraham Maslow, who developed the "hierarchy of needs" concept, put the desire for self-actualization atop the list of human needs—food, shelter, warmth, security, sense of belonging. I was pleased to discover that, unlike the world of psychologists who preceded him, Maslow was an optimist about human nature, interested in sources of happiness, rather than roots of unhappiness.

I am an optimist, and the more I read about Maslow and his work, the better it all sounded. As I considered his list of characteristics of a self-actualizer, I found myself there. Independent and resourceful, check; ever-present appreciation for life's gifts of sunset, flowers, majestic views, check; comfortable with solitude, check; a few close friends, rather than many superficial ones, check; profound interpersonal relationship, check. And the list goes on.

So, I'm a self-actualizer, and, for years, I embraced the concept. But today I wonder. It all seems too pat, a convenient way of rationalizing the choice I'd made to rebalance the career-motherhood equation in my life. Can self-actualization be so self-centered a motivation that it becomes selfishness? Can the independent spirit of a self-actualizer cause harm to others, especially those closest to you?

The question takes me to my father. Dad was a dotetcher; his was a specialized and creative role in an earlier world of color printing called lithography. He was proud of his work and brought home numerous coffee-table books on the scenic Northwest filled with photographs he had worked on in the color-processing stage of production. He was also proud to be an active member of his labor union. As a father of four daughters, he dreamed up the plan to uproot his young family from relatives in Ohio for a job in Oregon. Through the years I have had no reason to think that Mom was anything other than a willing partner. But now I wonder if the family story of an adventurous young couple with four little girls bravely heading west in a Chevy sedan pulling a small trailer is part mythology. In later years I began to realize how much Mom treasured her family connections back East, in contrast to Dad, who was cooler about his family ties. Surely, she felt some lingering pain in the separation from her close family upbringing.

Two years after the cross-country move, Dad took a job as an international vice president with the union and moved the family to Kansas City, Missouri. We returned to Portland two years later, and Dad went back to work as a dot-etcher. About a dozen years later, after I had graduated from college, married, had a baby, and left home, Dad once again moved the family, this time to Seattle for what he thought would be a better job. That job didn't turn out as Dad expected, and two years later the family was back in the Portland area. In subsequent years I learned that my younger sister, Robin, the sweetest, shyest, and most sensitive of all the daughters, who was pulled out of high school to finish her senior year in a new town, harbored a deep resentment toward Dad for the difficult and friendless year his career move forced upon her.

As I recount all these moves, I can't help but layer on top of them my own career moves and the decision to leave Matt and Tim in Boise with their father. I see my Dad's frequent moves as part of who I am, an adult who welcomes change and new challenges. A striver. But at what cost? Did my path leave Tim, like my sister Robin, with a deep hurt that was slow to heal?

In his retirement years, Dad continued to have it his way, spending day after day in his workshop making the small, scale-model hardwood cars he was so proud of, seldom indulging Mom's wishes to travel. She visited me and Bill occasionally, and I sensed a melancholy, probably depression, as her health declined, and Dad continued to make cars in his garage workshop.

At age seventy-eight, Mom was near death in a nursing home, and the family was gathering around her room at the end of a long hallway. With kind indulgence of staff, two younger sisters from out of town camped out with pillows and sleeping bags on the floor just outside the door to Mom's room. When time was near to say goodbye, Dad took Mom's hand and, with tears in his eyes, heaved a sigh and prepared to say something. The rest of us hushed and heard Dad's soft voice, "I love you, Foby." Never had I heard Dad utter the word *love* to a family member. Mom rallied briefly, showing a final hint of the spunk she passed on to her daughters, her voice faint, but clear: "It's about time." Sisters, with moist eyes and surprised smiles, exchanged wide-eyed glances.

I LOOK BACK ON ALL THOSE FAMILY MOVES AND WHAT I've come to think of as Mom's sad years and wonder what motivated my father. He was proud of supporting his family and worked many overtime hours to provide a good living for us. Typical of his generation, he was the patriarch and decision maker.

As my sisters and I creep past middle age, we gather every few years at a rental house on the Oregon coast for a sisters-only reunion. Conversation inevitably turns to Mom and Dad, including the various moves. I have been outspoken in my view that Dad was selfish and insensitive about the family disruptions he caused. Writing this has made me pause to consider whether my plan to leave the boys with Ken, thinking it would cause less disruption in their lives, is an unconscious reaction to the multiple family moves my sisters and I faced. If I see my father's actions as selfish, what about my own? I didn't drag my kids around the country; instead I left them behind.

I think of myself as a lot like Dad, including sharing many of the self-actualizer characteristics on Maslow's list. Dad was living out the role of the patriarch, a man of the fifties. And me? I'm a feminist of the seventies.

Did Maslow, who died in 1970, have mostly male achievers in mind as he studied sources of happiness and developed his theory of self-actualization? He once wrote that the specific desire for self-fulfillment will vary from person to person. "In one individual it may take the form of the desire to be an ideal mother...." And what, I now ask myself, if a young mother realizes her self-fulfillment desire is to be a journalist?

I KNOW THIS FOR SURE: MY WORK LIFE HAS BEEN ESSENtial to my sense of self. I am a better, smarter, happier person because of my career. I like to think that, for my sons, having a mother who found happiness in a personal relationship and success as a woman who went to work in a profession not all that friendly to females at the start is an important underpinning of who they are and what they value. Does it outweigh the tears and sadness they felt at all those good-byes and long absences? Only they can answer that question. That is their story. This has been mine.

EPILOGUE

Lake Pend Oreille
Summer, 2016

————————◆————————

"Is that Papa?" hollered a grandson from the front of the pontoon boat.

"Yep, that's Happy," said another.

"I guess the party's not over yet," said Matt. He had just begun to pick up towels, soda cans, and bags of chips to stow away for the boat ride back to our dock at Bottle Bay.

I live for the summers in my little portion of north Idaho. The season is short, but the days are long and full of activity, especially when my sons and grandsons and their wives and friends arrive for vacation. A day on a borrowed pontoon boat, a recent addition to our summer fun, was my favorite summer day. Bill and I have had a modest boat on Lake Pend Oreille for decades. We've pulled grandkids on water skis, kneeboards, and float tubes the size of a small sofa. I water skied until a pulled leg muscle ended the fun many years ago. More recently, when it's just us, Bill and I enjoy an evening booze cruise; we grab a bottle of wine, two plastic glasses, and a bag of chips, and off we go, slowly cruising near the shore, critiquing new construction, admiring handsome old cabins among the cedars and pines.

Family time on the pontoon boat is a totally different boating experience. Pontoon boats are flat and slow, ideal for parties. Matt and Tim; grandsons Sage, Riley, and Henry; Matt's wife, Andrea; and family friends and their three children hauled coolers, bags of food, paddle boards, and floats to the pontoon boat on the neighbor's dock. Bill would join us after work. We piled aboard and headed for Green Bay. On this day Ken's widow, Gail, joined us; Ken had died five months earlier. We were all remembering last summer when Grandpa Ken was with us, weakened by cancer, but still able to enjoy a day boating and floating in the water with his sons and grandsons. Late in the afternoon, when Bill's boat was spotted, and Matt announced the party would continue, a chorus of hoorays from the pontoon crowd filled the tranquil bay. The cheers were as much for the promise of staying longer as for Bill's arrival. The white and yellow runabout turned into Green Bay, where we had already spent the better part of the day. Sage and Henry, who first spotted the boat turning our way from far out in the lake, positioned themselves to help Bill tie up to the pontoon.

When Tim's first son, Sage, was born in 1998, I announced that Bill and I would be Papa and Nana, and so we were, also to Riley, who came along in 2002. Matt and Andrea's son, Henry, who was born the following year called his dad Papa. To avoid confusion, Bill soon became "Happy;" it stuck because he was, well, always happy.

"Here, Happy, have a beer," said Tim, handing Bill a Corona as he came aboard. "Your workday is over."

Green Bay, a secluded spot on Lake Pend Oreille where the calm water is made green by the reflection of pines and firs along the sandy shore, is protected on both sides by rock outcroppings. Just as I had every other year, as we eased into Green Bay, I gave a sigh of relief to once again find this near-perfect spot had few other visitors and an available buoy to tie onto.

Andrea tossed the stand-up paddle boards onto the water and soon paddled away from the boat. Standing at the front of the boat, bathed in sunshine, I watched her slim, bikini-clad figure glide through the water, remembering my own failed attempt on a stand-up paddle board several years earlier off the dock in Bottle Bay. It's not as easy as it looked, at least not for me.

"Let's go to the rocks," said Sage, jumping into the water to grab another board. Riley climbed on with him while Henry held onto the edge and pushed his cousins through the water to the cliff that frames the south side of the bay. My grandsons disappeared around the rocky entrance to a short trail that leads upwards to a point that juts out. They reappeared and stood for several seconds, looking down into the water, back to the pontoon, all the while working up their courage. I waved and gave them a thumbs-up. Then, one by one, they jumped into the water. I loved seeing their joy but took deep breaths to calm my nerves while watching. Jumping into the water like that would scare me to death. I like being in the water, though I'm not much of a swimmer. But, unlike my sons and grandsons, I have never, even as a youngster, had any daredevil impulses. Quite the opposite, in fact. I have a fear of heights and while I enjoy hiking, traversing narrow paths with steep drop-offs is a challenge for me. To me, the path always seems narrower and the drop-off steeper than it is to my hiking companions.

Once while hiking with Bill, my sister Becky, and her husband on Hawaii's Big Island, I surprised them all by stopping. I sat down, leaned hard against the hillside, as far away from the steep, deep drop-off as possible, and stared at the trail ahead; it seemed to stretch forever along the edge of the green chasm at my feet. "Sorry," I said. "I can't go any farther. Go on. I'll wait here."

I've come to terms with this 'fraidy cat me, but it seems to puzzle my family. My image among sisters and sons is as a competent, successful, even occasionally intimidating person. Intellectually I am quick, confident, and sometimes bold. Facing down angry readers of the newspaper's opinion pages is one thing; standing on the edge looking hundreds of feet down is quite another. One is an intellectual challenge, the other a physical reality that no amount of wit and smarts can change. Slowly, those close to me have come to realize—as I have—that as a hiker, I'm a coward.

Tim once surprised me by announcing he was going with friends to a place in Canada to harness up and bungee jump off a bridge into the river canyon below. I could barely watch the video he brought back to torment me.

From my earliest memories as a five-year-old moving with my family from Ohio to Oregon—all because my father had "seen the mountains"—I have felt an attachment to place and to landscapes. It's my family legacy. Once we settled in Oregon, it was the ocean and its sandy beaches that drew me. As a young adult in Boise, Idaho, I was attracted to the Boise River, which bisected the town and lured walkers and bikers, even back in the seventies, before today's development of miles of greenbelt and riverside parks. Seattle has more than its share of beautiful landscapes—Puget Sound, Lake Union, Lake Washington, and nearby forests, streams, and mountains. Oddly, however, I didn't develop the same connection to Seattle that I had to other places. I never tired of the wondrous view from the I-5 bridge on a sunny day with the Cascades to the east, the snow-capped Olympics to the west and water below in both directions, but the city did not attach itself to my heart. Despite living there for twenty years, I always felt like a transient; it was a place to work and enjoy the urban life, but I never felt a timeless sense of belonging.

After moving to Seattle in 1981, Bill and I often returned to Idaho to vacation with friends, always on a lake. Eventually we began staying at another friend's waterfront cabin near Sandpoint on Lake Pend Oreille. Matt lived in town with his father until he graduated from high school in 1984, and Tim liked to return for visits. Justin, who was then living in California with his Mom, was eager to vacation anywhere with his dad. Friends and colleagues in Seattle thought we were nuts. So far! A six-hour drive! There is so much to do and see near Seattle! They seemed to think that nothing but desert and uncivilized life existed on the other side of the Cascades. An attachment to place is like falling in love with a person; it can't be explained with logic. I loved the lake and enjoyed the small-town charms of Sandpoint. By 1987, comfortably settled into our jobs in Seattle, Bill and I decided to look for vacation property. We soon bought a rundown cabin overlooking Bottle Bay and the forested hillside across the water. To the right from our waterfront we could see the bay widen into Lake Pend Oreille and a view of the Selkirk Mountains with telltale ribbons of Schweitzer ski runs.

Today our Bottle Bay cabin is as close as Bill and I come to having a family home. It is filled with more than thirty years of memories: The spot on the north wall where Bill shot a nail through his hand during our early remodel. The exterior doors I painted red with help from my sister, Becky.

The large rocks Tim helped me place on the front slope have been removed for a more recent landscape upgrade and await their next use. The deck Justin helped Bill build has been replaced, but the backyard fence and patio created by Matt and Andrea are still there, along with an aging teak bench and small table, ideal for a cup of tea in the warmth of the morning sun.

It was a dump when we bought it—a house that today would be called a mow-down, small and cramped. Friends visited soon after the purchase, and the wife was too stout to fit into the tiny shower. Fix-up started at the waterfront, using big rocks instead of concrete to make a natural barrier for the lake lapping against the land. My father put his woodworking skills to use designing the short stairway from the narrow lane that separates the house from the waterfront strip. Dad is gone but his stairs still stand. We soon remodeled and expanded, changing the roofline to open it up toward the lake, finishing the exterior with redwood-stained cedar, and adding a red metal roof. It was transformed into *our cabin:* a place that felt like home, where our kids could visit and our often-fractured family could feel whole. A place to share with friends. A place for the evening tradition called *la passeggiata,* walking (or biking or skateboarding) to the end of the road and back. A place to build a future around.

Inside, the main cabin area is open and airy and serves as both living and dining room, separated from the kitchen to the back only by a counter and stove top. A forest-green carpet provides a soft contrast to wood-paneled ceiling and walls. Wooden blinds hang in the large windows across the west-facing front. Above the window wall we installed a shelf the length of the room where we display a collection of antique toys, a chalkboard for welcoming guests, an old camera, a guitar with a broken string, and a green street sign that says "Cameron." Near one end is a sneaker signed by U.S. Senator Patty Murray, who ran for office in the early nineties in Washington State. While other political writers in the state dismissed her as "the lady in tennis shoes," I took her seriously and wrote several favorable columns about her. As I write this, she is still in the U.S. Senate, well respected by her colleagues, and popular in her home state.

The cabin was more than a vacation home; for Bill it became therapy. Television news was changing as consultants gained more influence and newsrooms were expected to bend to new ways of presenting the news—shorter stories, more cops and crime, fewer reporter-driven investigative pieces. Bill was by then a newsroom supervisor and not all that happy trying to manage a roomful of cocky television reporters resistant to change.

One Friday past midnight we pulled into the cabin driveway; we sat in the car for a moment, breathing deeply, listening to the silence. "Must be a bright moon," I said, noticing the silvery glow outlining the trees. "Let's go in," said Bill. "We can look at the moonlight from inside." He nudged me with one hand, opened his car door with the other. Arriving at the cabin after working all day, trying to get away before six, but rarely managing that, produced instant, full-body relaxation. Stiffness in shoulders, neck, arms, and legs, cramped from the long drive, eased as I opened the door and walked into the cabin. I turned on the Tiffany-style lamp hanging over the funky, round antique dining table. I liked the soft, romantic glow of the lamp that enhanced the room's faint woodsy smell, and the lingering odor of wood smoke from previous fires in the stove. It

looked and smelled like home. Bill opened the liquor cabinet. These late arrivals always warranted a nightcap.

"What's your mood tonight, port or scotch?"

"I'm in a port mood," I said, "how about you?" He
poured two glasses of twelve -year-old tawny port, and we
sat close together on the sofa, facing the wood-burning
stove. Too late to start a fire, and too chilly to take off our
jackets, we snuggled. "What's tomorrow's project?" I asked.
We had talked most of the way across the state about his
aggravations at work and the latest frustration with a com-
plaining reporter. Once we entered the cabin, we left that
behind. Bill's head was in a new space, cabin space. He
went over the list of possible projects: fix the light and fan
in the downstairs room, repair treads of various decks and
steps, move a pile of rocks. We were always moving rocks
from somewhere to somewhere else. "Take a walk and chat
with the neighbors," I added. Once Bill got into project
mode, he could spend the whole day at it. Every upgrade,
no matter how small, and every neighbor who became a
friend only deepened our attachment to the cabin. We didn't
imagine it then, but Bottle Bay would become an attachment that altered the trajectory of our professional lives.

The seeds of that change were planted on a cool, sunny
spring day in 1991, during a long walk on the John Wayne
Trail east of Snoqualmie Summit when Bill, then forty-four,
surprised me. "What would you think about me going to
law school?" I knew he had been searching for something
else to do with his life, but this was unexpected. "Interesting,"
was all I could manage. We continued to walk as I absorbed
the idea. I could sense his seriousness. After a short silence,
I stopped and turned to him. "Where did this idea came
from? How would we make it work?"

Coincidently, I also had an idea kicking around my head that I wanted to talk about on our walk. At that time Harvard and Michigan offered fellowship programs for midcareer journalists. A nine-month break from the daily grind of newspapering was appealing to me after more than twenty years of working with only two- or three-week vacation breaks, but I had not explored a fellowship in any depth. I thought of it as something I might apply for in the next three to five years. I mentioned it to Bill, and as often happened with us, new ideas about our future sparked intense mental energy and streams of consciousness as our thoughts raced ahead to what-ifs and what-about-this, or that. Our conversation that day on the walk and during the car ride home changed the middle years of our personal and professional lives together, much as leaving the boys and moving to Rochester had changed the early years.

At the heart of the new plan was our attachment to the Bottle Bay cabin and a dream of eventually retiring in Sandpoint. A law career was portable; Bill could practice law in Sandpoint as easily as Seattle. Instead of taking a break for a fellowship, I would continue working, retire early—at fifty-eight—and have many years to embrace the life I coveted as a civic volunteer in my favorite small town. Thrilled about the possibility this might really happen, I easily let go of my fellowship dream. I grinned and announced to Bill, "Your law degree will be my early retirement plan."

Bill earned his law degree in 1995, at age fifty, and worked for the King County Prosecutor until July of 2001, when our new life in Sandpoint began. By early 2002 he had started a solo law practice in Sandpoint. About four years earlier, knowing our plans were firm, we had purchased twenty-five acres of forested and open land with a stream only five miles from our Bottle Bay cabin and eighteen miles from Sandpoint. Early investments in Starbucks and Microsoft made it possible to build a large garage and shop building and later a six-hundred-square-foot guest cottage that we would use until we built a real house among the trees on a ridge above, overlooking a small lake. Within a year or two we had a dog, chickens, a garden, and a greenhouse. A friend in Seattle once asked what I missed most about the city. "Miss the most?" I paused. "I don't miss *anything*, so there is no 'most.'"

WE WERE STILL IN SEATTLE WHEN THE FIRST GRANDSON was born. Bill and I were in the hospital waiting room, a windowless nondescript room of pale hospital green with chairs covered in gray plastic. A few other anxious people, all strangers, also waited quietly. The room fades away when a mother experiences for the first time the exquisite tenderness of witnessing her son fall in love with his new baby. I saw Tim come through the double doors of the delivery room and down the short hall, holding the swaddled baby gently in his arms, staring into his face. He looked up at me, smiled, his brown eyes soft with moisture. "Here he is," he said, almost a murmur, as if anything more would break the spell. He held the baby out for me to take in my arms. I held him and looked at Tim and the baby. "Beautiful," I whispered: Tim, the baby, and the moment.

Tim was thrilled to be a father, and I was delighted to be a grandmother, spending as much time as possible with the new parents and their baby. Tim's happiness over fatherhood was soon interrupted by heartbreak. Sage was barely walking when I learned the marriage was in trouble. I was thrust back into a familiar pattern of worrying about Tim, wondering what my role was, how and whether I could make a difference for him. And now there was that roly-poly, brown-eyed toddler to worry about also.

Before he was married Tim had enrolled in a culinary arts program at South Seattle Community College. He had no trouble finding jobs, and from time to time he also found romance on the job. A year or so after his divorce, he began dating a waitress he met at the restaurant. Eventually they had a child, Riley, lived together for several years but never married, and eventually separated. By this time, I was in Sandpoint, traveling frequently to Seattle to see Tim and his boys.

All this time, Matt was doing what he'd done almost since he was eleven—raising himself. He moved to Hood River and found work to support his windsurfing habit—building houses and later sail boards. He met Andrea in Hood River, and it was love at first meeting for me and Bill. We anxiously waited out the years of their romance, their joint house purchase in Hood River, and, finally, their engagement one holiday season while staying at the Bottle Bay cabin. The following summer, 1997, they were married overlooking Puget Sound. They moved to Portland and went back to college. Matt became a mechanical engineer, and Andrea has a career in marketing.

On my sixtieth birthday in 2003, Matt called to announce I had a new grandson, Henry. I left the next day for Portland. There, in the craftsman-style house they were remodeling, I watched Matt changing the baby's diaper. I noticed how expert he seemed already, both gentle and confident as he pulled the diaper snug, telling tiny Henry in a low voice what a great kid he was. This son, so different from his brother, unsentimental in contrast to Tim's sensitivity, was falling in love with his son in his own beautiful way.

Tim and Matt are children of divorced parents. Tim's serious relationships have been with women whose parents were divorced, as were Andrea's parents. That's a lot of dysfunction in the lives and relationships of my sons. Matt and Andrea were older and more mature when they married. Their wait to have a child seemed to me as if they were making sure they were solid as a couple and would not repeat the family pattern. Tim, eager to create his own family, plunged right in. His life has stabilized, and today my grandsons have fabulous fathers, men who are attentive and loving.

THAT DAY ON THE PONTOON BOAT ENDED BACK AT Bottle Bay, as do all our summer days together. A simple dinner, dockside activities—jumping, swimming, paddle boarding, kayaking—and, finally, *la passeggiata* as the sun set behind the forested green hill across the bay, giving our small world a peachy-pink evening glow for a few splendid moments.

ACKNOWLEDGMENTS

This book would not have happened without the guidance of faculty in the Pacific University MFA program. I am particularly indebted to Debra Gwartney who prodded me down the sometimes-rocky road from journalist to memoirist, and to Scott Korb who seemed to understand me, and my story better than I did. I am grateful to fellow students who appreciated my story and helped make it better with their insightful comments. One stands out for her detailed contributions: Amy Paterson's pages of notes and editing suggestions on my final manuscript were my guide through the post-MFA revision process. Sadly, Amy died of cancer before I had a chance to thank her.

Others who contributed include Kathy Triesch, a former colleague at the Seattle Times with a well-deserved reputation as a fine editor. A long-time friend and writer Lois Melina read the manuscript at a late stage and gave me numerous suggestions that made the story work better. Thanks to Cate Huisman for the final eagle-eye editing task that only a real professional can provide. Any errors that remain are mine, not other readers.

Also, thanks to my sisters, Judy, Becky, Jenny, Robin, Chris, and Susan, for a lifetime of caring friendship. What rare good luck it is to have a homemade support group. And, of course, endless gratitude for Bill, whose love and laughter brightens every day.

About the Author

Mindy Cameron, a retired journalist, lives with her husband on rural acreage near Sandpoint, Idaho. She is a former editorial page editor at The Seattle Times and managing editor at the Lewiston Morning Tribune. She also worked at the Idaho Statesman in Boise and for public television in Boise and Rochester, New York.

Shortly after moving to Idaho in 2001 Mindy and her husband, Bill Berg, founded the Panhandle Alliance for Education (PAFE), a nonprofit that supports local public schools. She was elected to the school board and served 11 years. She also served on the Idaho Humanities Council and the Inland Northwest Community Foundation (now Innovia Foundation). In 2018, she received her MFA in creative writing from Pacific University.